PRINCE2

OGC
Office of Government Commerce

London: TSO

Published by TSO (The Stationery Office) and available from:

Online
www.tso.co.uk/bookshop

Mail, Telephone, Fax & E-mail
TSO
PO Box 29, Norwich, NR3 1GN
Telephone orders/General enquiries: 0870 600 5522
Fax orders: 0870 600 5533
E-mail: book.orders@tso.co.uk
Textphone 0870 240 3701

TSO Shops
123 Kingsway, London, WC2B 6PQ
020 7242 6393 Fax 020 7242 6394
68-69 Bull Street, Birmingham B4 6AD
0121 236 9696 Fax 0121 236 9699
9-21 Princess Street, Manchester M60 8AS
0161 834 7201 Fax 0161 833 0634
16 Arthur Street, Belfast BT1 4GD
028 9023 8451 Fax 028 9023 5401
18-19 High Street, Cardiff CF10 1PT
029 2039 5548 Fax 029 2038 4347
71 Lothian Road, Edinburgh EH3 9AZ
0870 606 5566 Fax 0870 606 5588

TSO Accredited Agents
(see Yellow Pages)

and through good booksellers

First published 2002

ISBN 0 11 330896 5

OGC – the Office of Government Commerce – is an office of HM Treasury. Set up in 2000, it incorporates the Central Computer and Telecommunications Agency (CCTA), which no longer operates as a separate agency.

The OGC is now the authority for best practice in commercial activities in UK Government, combining a number of separate functions with related aims.

OGC will build on the popular guidance developed by the former CCTA and others, working with organisations internationally to develop and share business and practitioner guidance within a world-class best practice framework.

Printed in the United Kingdom for The Stationery Office.

CONTENTS

FOREWORD

Successful management of business change is a priority for today's organisations in order to remain effective and competitive. It is crucial to manage the inherent risks associated with projects and to effectively implement change and innovation in a rapidly altering environment.

PRINCE2 embodies many years of good practice in project management and provides a flexible and adaptable approach to suit all projects.

This guide is intended to fill some of the areas not specifically covered by the PRINCE2 method, by highlighting the importance of managing the 'soft' issues. These issues may be an impediment to the smooth running of projects so have to be anticipated and managed as risks. Having the right people to manage and contribute to projects at all levels is a key factor in the successful delivery of the project's end products and in achieving the business objectives.

I commend this *People Issues and PRINCE2* guide to you and hope that it will help you to implement PRINCE2 in your organisation and to achieve the successful outcome your business expects.

Bob Assirati
Executive Director
Office of Government Commerce

ACKNOWLEDGEMENTS

OGC gratefully acknowledges the contribution made by John Fisher and David Small of Xansa to the creation of this publication.

In addition, the input of the following individuals, who acted as reviewers, is recognised:

Brian Swales (The Learning Habit)

Marion Thackwray (Balance Consulting)

Colin Bentley

Alan Ferguson (AFA Project Management)

Bethan Hubbard (Scottish Parliament – user)

Stewart Barrie (user)

1
PEOPLE, RISKS AND THE BUSINESS CASE

Introduction

The success or failure of a project rests on, among other things, the Project Manager's ability to manage discrepancies between the plan and reality. PRINCE2's framework and basis are geared to allowing Project Managers to do this, in part through an effective and accurate planning process. Planning, though, is predictive and, alongside the weather, people probably rank as the single most unpredictable element of any project.

Feedback from users of PRINCE2 has regularly identified this single issue – planning around the human input to a project – as the most difficult aspect of the PRINCE2 method to implement successfully. It is the area most likely to generate problems for a project. Because PRINCE2 does not encompass people management, however, there is no particular 'PRINCE2 approach' to people issues and, therefore, no guidance has been published under the PRINCE2 banner on this subject. Because the management of issues arising from 'human factors' can have a profound effect on a project nonetheless, the Office of Government Commerce (OGC) decided to commission this publication. It aims to help Project Managers:

● identify the likely points within a project at which particular so-called 'people issues' can arise

● be aware of the possible effects of some of these issues

● plan for these issues in order to mitigate some of the associated effects

● put forward a range of accepted management approaches and remedies

● learn from the experience of others through examples and case studies.

Like PRINCE2 itself, this guidance is generic as opposed to sector-specific and should hold true for almost any type of PRINCE2 project: human nature and behaviour remain remarkably constant whatever the peculiarities or nuances of the project context. The planning and coping strategies set out in this guide cannot guarantee that the people issues concerned will not arise or present problems but, at the very least, a Project Manager who has read the book will be forewarned and, hopefully, forearmed.

1.1 PRINCE2 and people

Readers familiar with *Managing Successful Projects with PRINCE2* (OGC, 2002) will be aware that apart from the management team in the organisation component, there is little discussion of people, their management or the problems that could arise. PRINCE2 recognises that there are certain aspects of project management that are well covered by existing and proven methods, including people management techniques such as motivation, delegation and team leadership. These are therefore excluded from the PRINCE2 manual.

There are many examples of ordinary teams in both project and non-project environments producing extraordinary results. In their extensive study of major projects, Morris and Hough (1987) found the following 'human factors' were essential for success:

- the recognition and demonstration of effective leadership
- the deployment of competent people
- the maintenance of effective communication
- the choice of appropriate power style
- the recognition that people are human and less than perfect.

One of their many conclusions was that 'the way people's qualities can be maximised to the project's benefit is ultimately where success or failure begins'.

Whichever project or study is referred to, a common factor in all cases will be the way in which people are treated both individually and as part of a team.

If people issues are left unattended there could be a resultant lack of:

- enthusiasm to complete work and perform at the highest level
- respect for other team members in terms of their needs, abilities and well-being
- development of workable solutions through sharing of information and consultation with peers and management.

This could lead to lower productivity or, even worse, project failure.

Projects appear to suffer from people problems just as day-to-day work can. Projects, however, have characteristics that make problems more acute. Their time sensitivity tends to be greater, so the pressure and intensity may be higher and the deliverables can be more visible than the outputs of the day-to-day operations. Also, the fact that they are often cross-cutting or cross-functional means that the impact of politics, power-games and other agendas can be more powerful. For projects the context is a huge factor too, much more so than in 'business as usual'. The next section looks at this in more detail.

1.2 People and projects

An explanation as to why projects appear to suffer from people problems could be that working on projects is full of paradoxes and apparent contradictions. Some examples include:

- not having enough time and/or spending too much time on a project
- conflict between planning and the need to get on with work
- the stress and challenge of unique and innovative work
- the need to deliver change, and people's resistance to that change.

Other reasons could be due to some of the characteristics of a project. This section looks at four aspects of projects that afford some understanding of why people problems can arise:

- the Business Case
- current business environment
- organisational environment
- previous project success.

1.2.1 The Business Case

All projects require a Business Case. Moreover, a project without a Business Case should not be started and a project with a Business Case that changes during the life of the project should be reviewed. This is done to ensure that the business benefits will still be delivered after project completion and is the key tenet of the PRINCE2 approach.

After all the financial analysis has been completed, the Business Case can, as Figure 1.1 shows, have one of the following possible outcomes:

- viable
- not viable
- grey.

The strength of the Business Case – or otherwise – influences every other aspect of the project, including the people, how they behave, their management, motivation and perceived success or failure.

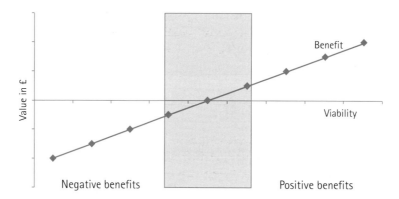

Figure 1.1 Possible outcomes of project viability (positive, negative and grey)

1.2.1.1 Viable projects

This is the simplest of cases. If the project is viable then authorisation for continuing with the project should be gained from the Project Board. No inherent people problems arise from the Business Case if it is auspicious in this way.

1.2.1.2 Not viable/Grey area projects

These projects should not be started or continued without more work to understand fully the business benefits that may be delivered as a result of the project. However, the organisation may still demand the project to be initiated and subsequently delivered. To meet the 'viability' criterion the Project Manager may be under pressure to:

- pad the Business Case with a significant number of intangible benefits, or
- claim benefits that do not exist.

This pressure can come from two sources, the users and the suppliers. It is worth bearing in mind that:

- users may be desperate for the project to continue as they see it as essential for their needs, and
- suppliers may also want the project to continue; for example, a project may result in a lower failure rate for systems or reduce the amount of time spent supporting users.

Putting a strong case at this time in favour of not proceeding may lose the confidence and support of the various players should the Project Board decide to continue the project. It is essential, therefore, that the Project Manager understands the reasons and counter-arguments which make this project grey or not viable and look for diplomatic ways to defend 'no go' recommendations without alienating the key players. If the project proceeds nonetheless, its very circumstances in terms of viability may have an adverse effect on those involved with it, especially if the team is aware of a creaky Business Case and its implications for the likely outcome.

1.2.2 Current business environment

Alvin Toffler, in his book *Future Shock* (1971), described an organisation that within a two-year period bought eight companies and sold off five in an attempt to consolidate and trade off troublesome components. The scope of that book was the period 1967 to 1969. Today, in the first years of the 21st century, things are not much different. Businesses are under significant pressures as shown in Figure 1.2.

Figure 1.2 Pressures and influences on business

Consideration of the business environment is an important issue that affects how teams perform. In a fluid or dynamic environment, taking on a long-term project may be considered unwise and may require extra thought as to the impact on the team. In this type of environment, team motivation and therefore productivity can be impacted by:

●   constant mergers and de-mergers, especially where staff shrinkage may be involved

●   frequent cancellation of projects due to either the threat of takeover or actual takeover

- rate of change exceeding the rate of progress, especially when it involves reworking products already reviewed and delivered.

Even in environments that are considered stable or more resistant to change, there are still pressures to consider. These may include:

- the need to reform and modernise
- the ageing of the workforce and subsequent succession planning
- the problems of introducing new staff with new ideas.

When working in this type of environment team motivation can be impacted by:

- buy-in to solutions
- rate of change to solutions
- constraining solutions to minimise the impact on end users.

1.2.3 Organisational environment

Project Managers have to work with many different types of organisational structures including:

- functional
- project-focused
- matrix.

Functional organisations have a traditional organisational structure. A member of staff will have one clear superior and will work in a team grouped by speciality, for example, marketing, networks, finance, etc. In this type of environment Project Managers tend to find difficulties when managing cross-functional projects due to the inability to agree overall leadership within the various groups. As a result there needs to be significant investment from senior management to lead, direct and prioritise work and resolve issues.

Project-focused organisations are those that as a norm work in mixed project teams, usually as a commercial supplier to other organisations. In this environment, management by projects is a key feature of the way change is managed and Project Managers are recognised as specialists who bring the various diverse skills together, removing the problems faced by the functional groups discussed earlier.

Matrix management is usually found in organisations that have functional structures but which recognise the need for project-focused teams. It is in these organisations that the Project Manager needs to be aware of the tendency of some line managers and staff to revert back to functional working and protectionism of the functional structures. This can have an impact on product delivery during the life of the project when securing and retaining both technical staff and users.

1.2.4 Previous project success

Closely related to both the organisation's structure and business environment is the culture of successful delivery – or otherwise. How successful is the organisation at delivering projects? An organisation's track record can have a bearing on key 'human' aspects of subsequent projects, not least in terms of a positive or negative motivational impact. Indeed a track record may exist for reasons that subsequent projects need to be aware of.

Project-focused organisations should have little difficulty demonstrating project success with evidence coming from documents like Lessons Learned Reports, End Project Reports and Post-Project Reviews. Projects closed down prematurely due to problems with disappearing business benefits, i.e. no clear business need to continue, can still be considered in this context to be successful in that the organisation has shown a significant level of maturity in both recognising a problem and dealing with it.

Working in an environment where there is a history of repeated project failure, the need for this historical research becomes more acute. The question that needs to be addressed is 'What made that project a failure?' Here the Project Manager is looking for clues as to how the organisation performed as opposed to the products being delivered. This will include the performance and behaviour of the Project Board, project team and Project Manager.

1.3 Summary

Some characteristics of projects can cause people to behave differently on projects than in day-to-day business.

The positive message is that, with an understanding of the way different environments change people's behaviours on projects, the successful Project Manager can resolve issues that prevent teams producing extraordinary results.

Project Managers that have an insight and understanding of the people side of project management will be able to get more out of their project teams. To an extent this may be a function of a Project Manager's 'emotional intelligence' vis-à-vis their team and, as such, partly intuitive. Such perception can be heightened, however, through awareness, anticipation, exemplification and practice.

Before looking in more detail at where PRINCE2 interfaces directly with people factors and how these may be managed, the next chapter looks at some established theories concerning people and their management. Understanding basic elements of human behaviour in a business context is the first step towards being able to predict and manage it on a project.

2
MANAGEMENT THEORIES

2.1 Introduction

This chapter reviews some of the more common theories of people and team working and how they can help illuminate and address the people issues on a project.

The first of these is leadership style since the Project Manager's own conduct of themselves and the project brings a considerable influence to bear on the behaviour of others involved in an undertaking. Project Managers need to have a variety of management styles at their disposal and knowledge of which style is appropriate in each circumstance.

2.2 Leadership style

Scottish psychologist Douglas McGregor (1960) said that there were two extremes in the way that leaders perceived the people working for them. These perceptions strongly influence a leader's behaviour.

McGregor called these extremes Theory X and Theory Y leaders.

The Theory X leader believes that people must be made to work otherwise they will not do it. Such people have little ambition to progress and succeed. This leader will instruct, drive and monitor performance regularly and is almost completely 'production centred', usually adopting an autocratic style.

- McGregor's X worker
    - is lazy
    - has to be forced to work
    - has little ambition
    - dislikes work
    - wants security
- McGregor's Y worker
    - enjoys work
    - responds to challenge
    - looks for job satisfaction
    - is self-motivated

Figure 2.1 McGregor's Theory X and Theory Y workers

The Theory Y leader, on the other hand, is much more 'employee centred', being of the belief that people are essentially self-motivated. Here the leadership style is more of a democratic approach.

Neither model is completely right, but some team workers exhibit predominantly Theory X characteristics and others predominantly Theory Y characteristics.

This can even vary according to the work situation. For example, even the most self-motivated people have been known to shirk unpleasant jobs. The Project Manager will need to be aware that as trust develops and experience increases with each team member the leadership style may well change from autocratic to democratic through to free rein. These styles are explained in more detail below.

Figure 2.2 Basic leadership styles

According to McGregor, there are three basic leadership styles:

- autocratic (do it my way)
- democratic (do it our way)
- free rein (do it your way).

These terms should not imply that one is better than the other. Each has benefits and disadvantages depending on the situation, the other parties and the way the style is carried off. People often think that autocratic is bad – this is not necessarily so.

Consider three different situations:

- an emergency (e.g. an emergency evacuation of a building)
- a meeting or brainstorming session
- routine work.

Consider two different types of team member:

- bright/experienced/able
- less bright/inexperienced/slow.

Now, considering the situations and the people, the most appropriate leadership style will vary for each of the given scenarios.

Situation	Leadership style
Emergency	Autocratic (people look for a strong, decisive hand in an emergency).
Meeting/brainstorm	Democratic (too much direction and authority stifles creative contribution and too little results in anarchy).
Routine	Free rein for the bright/experienced people. Autocratic for the slow/inexperienced people. Democratic for the 'in-between' people.

As the leader of the project, the Project Manager is responsible for coaxing the required input from the team in the time available and to the quality agreed. Whatever the management style displayed, the Project Manager's success in achieving the desired project outcome can hinge on whether the team is motivated to do the job. Not all aspects of the team's motivation will be within the Project Manager's control but they need to understand where they can make an impact and how.

2.3 Motivation of the team member

2.3.1 Describing motivation

Frederick Herzberg, an American psychologist, asked 200 professional engineers and accountants what events in their work resulted in a marked increase or decrease in their job satisfaction (Herzberg *et al*, 1959).

He found that motivation factors for these professional people could be categorised into positive and negative motivators (see Figure 2.3). Positive motivators are those which, when they are right, will increase motivation levels. Thus achievement, recognition and challenge can all increase job satisfaction and levels of productivity, quality and creativity. Negative motivators or 'hygiene factors', however, are those things which, when they are wrong, can demotivate. Thus a lack of security, a bad working environment and insufficient money, will reduce job satisfaction and motivation levels.

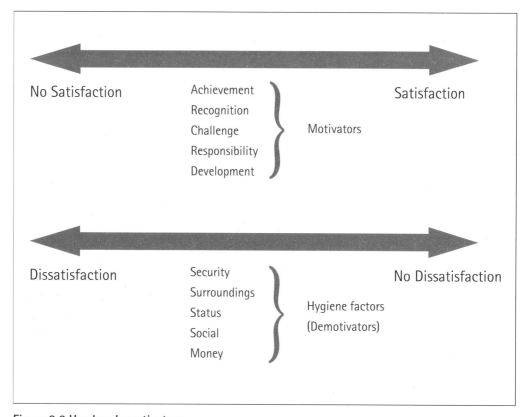

Figure 2.3 Herzberg's motivators

In practical terms, this means that people are generally unlikely to be motivated if the hygiene factors are wrong.

Herzberg said that what makes people happy and motivated at work is what they do and what makes people unhappy and demotivated at work is the environment (in its widest sense) in which they do it.

Project team members, therefore, are unlikely to be motivated by challenging work if their security is threatened. The message is, get the hygiene factors right first and then concentrate on the motivators.

In expounding his theory, Herzberg came up with some interesting subsidiary ideas. He suggested that people should be treated according to the way they actually are, not the way you want them to be. Criticism of a worker who is not showing the desired attitude is unlikely to achieve much beyond a lack of respect. Many failed projects are littered with cases of people who are unhappy because the Project Manager tried to force them to do things they felt were beyond their competence or inconsistent with their career direction.

Herzberg viewed motivation as a function of ability and opportunity. In other words, there is no point issuing a challenge to somebody without giving them the tools to do the job. One of these tools is training. The Project Manager may provide the opportunity, but must also ensure that the ability is there, otherwise demotivation will probably result from the frustration of failure.

Short-term improvements in performance can be achieved by threat or reward as Herzberg observed. To illustrate this, the reader should consider whether they would be motivated to do a job by a vast sum of money and also whether they would be motivated to do something for someone who threatened them with a gun. In both cases the answer will probably be 'yes'. So why not constantly use threat and reward? The problem is that these motivators would have to be applied at an increasing intensity in order for them to remain effective. A good example of this is the company-supplied car. Many people without a company car would be prepared to work very hard to get one, but those same people would be unlikely to continue to work at that level once they have got the car. Some new system of reward would need to be devised. In other words 'A reward once given becomes a right'.

Similarly, threats need to be kept up if they are to continue to be effective, but a possible negative outcome of a system of threats is the 'revenge psychology' syndrome. This is where an employee gets their own back on the project or organisation by acts of non-cooperation or even sabotage.

2.3.2 The motivation cycle

Herzberg's theory (Kolb and Fry, 1975) can be expressed as a virtuous cycle of motivation, which illustrates how ongoing personal development is nourished by renewing the motivators with each successful cycle.

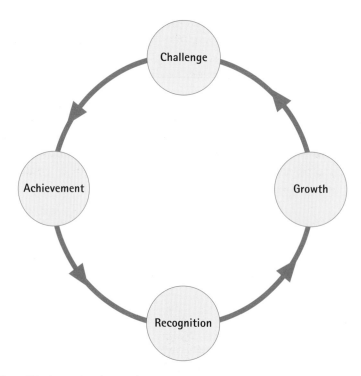

Figure 2.4 Kolb and Fry's motivation cycle

An initial challenge (within a worker's capabilities) is given; project management assists in the accomplishment of the challenge, leading to a sense of achievement.

This is recognised by project management, i.e. the accomplishment is noticed and a reaction given. The challenge, achievement and recognition stages contribute to a sense of growth. The worker's skills have been increased and self-confidence maintained. The person is ready for the next challenge.

PRINCE2 clearly gels with this approach by providing a clear and agreed definition of the initial challenge in the form of Work Packages and Product Descriptions. Proper planning based upon this can ensure that the resources (especially time) required to meet the challenge are rationally set and that the challenge is achievable.

The Product Description also ensures that the measures of acceptability (quality criteria) are agreed beforehand and can be used to assess completion. This gives the product builder a sense of satisfaction when the job is completely finished and it allows project management to know whether (and when) to give appropriate recognition.

The proper monitoring of progress against plans provides project management with a vehicle for assessing headway and providing encouragement along the way, if necessary.

The use of PRINCE2 as a vehicle for the employment of Herzberg's positive motivators is effective in keeping motivation levels high with the majority of people in a professional environment. The Project Manager must also remember, however, that the hygiene factors must always be kept appropriate to the situation.

Herzberg is persuasive in many ways, but is rather inflexible. What the theory takes little account of is the range of factors that motivate people, depending on the different situations that they find their lives in. Highly individualised motivators are not always practical for an organisation to accommodate and it remains the case that a 'one size fits all' approach is the most prevalent. A certain amount of demotivation arising from some element of an employee's role and conditions is, therefore, the norm.

2.3.3 People's needs

Maslow's (1954) hierarchy of human needs has, as its basis, the idea that the same person will be motivated by different factors or needs, according to the things that are preoccupying them at the time. This preoccupation is determined by what's going on in their life.

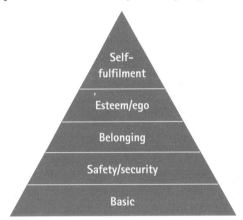

Figure 2.5 Maslow's hierarchy of needs

At the bottom level, people are motivated by the need to survive. If someone is drowning, they are only motivated towards staying alive. If life itself is not threatened, then people are motivated by the need for safety and security, e.g. keeping their job, house, etc. The next level is one of belonging – i.e. not to be lonely or rejected – to be part of a group or team and not be isolated. If the lower three levels are satisfied, then people begin to be motivated by things that are potentially more valuable to the organisation that employs them. The fourth level is about the needs of the ego and the esteem of others. People in a professional environment who are motivated at this level will usually work hard to build and keep their reputation for competence and hard work. The topmost level is about self-fulfilment or realisation of personal development. The person at this level is most likely to be concerned with the pursuit of personal excellence and the pursuit of the vision of what they, as an individual, want to be in their life. Organisations can therefore boost the project's chances of a positive outcome by ensuring that these three lowest levels of need are satisfied. Conversely, if workers are insecure or isolated, projects may suffer and there may be little the Project Manager can do about it.

2.4 Leadership style and project teams

2.4.1 Balancing the team and the individual

John Adair (1983, 1986, 1997), who developed his concept of action centred leadership at the British Army officer training college at Sandhurst, said that an effective leader had to balance three separate and often incompatible needs:

- project needs, i.e. the work that has to be done
- team needs, e.g. team spirit
- individual needs, e.g. the human need for recognition.

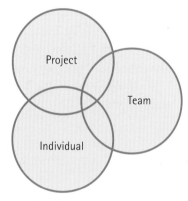

Figure 2.6 Adair's action centred leadership

Some of the project needs include clearly defined and agreed objectives, possibly as specified in the PRINCE2 Project Brief or Project Initiation Document. These are a vital prerequisite to the derivation of proper plans and work schedules, showing who does what, when and how.

The team aspects that the leader should satisfy revolve around communication. Involvement, creativity and consultation (i.e. a democratic style) all contribute towards the building of a robust team spirit. This can mean, however, that satisfaction of the team needs is not always compatible with those of the project. These facets of communication take time and time may be limited.

The needs of the individual also must be satisfied. An understanding of the motivational theories shows that all of the Herzberg motivators are in place and imply close attention on the part of the leader. This close attention could be, of course, incompatible with team working and the project needs.

The essence of good leadership, according to Adair, is to balance the three needs and not be too task-, team- or individual-oriented. In a matrix management environment, i.e. in a project environment, effective leadership is vital. The pay-off is improved productivity. Leadership, therefore, is partly about showing trust, loyalty, honesty and respect for individuals. Showing confidence and belief are crucial (even if it is not always felt), as is commitment to the job.

Good leaders also understand their people, what makes them tick and what they want out of their job.

Varying one's leadership style, according to the people and the situation, is important. Looking at the disparate needs of the project, team and individual and balancing those needs with the style of leadership is useful. In the final analysis though, the reasons why people follow leaders are essentially selfish and as soon as these reasons fade, so does the leader's ability and effectiveness.

2.4.2 Creating the perfect team

Meredith Belbin (1993, 1994) of the Henley Management Centre completed research into teams and team roles over the course of 10 years. The result was the identification of 'team roles' which showed that different people had different strengths in different types of activity and that, in a given environment, some combinations of roles worked better than others.

For each of the team roles, Belbin documented their typical features, positive qualities and allowable weaknesses. An allowable weakness is one that facilitates the strengths associated with a given team role and does not imply a need for correction.

Table 2.1 Belbin's team roles

Team type	Team role	Typical features	Positive qualities	Allowable weaknesses
Implementer	Good organiser who turns ideas into practical actions.	Conservative, dutiful and predictable. Disciplined, reliable and efficient.	Organising ability. Common sense; hard-working.	Lack of flexibility. Slow to respond to new possibilities.

Team type	Team role	Typical features	Positive qualities	Allowable weaknesses
Co-ordinator	Clarifies goals, co-ordinates, promotes decision-making.	Calm, self-confident, controlled.	Promotes decision-making, clarifies goals. Strong sense of objectives.	Can be seen as manipulative. Delegates personal work.
Shaper	Forces things along, shapes team's efforts. Identifies relationships between issues.	Outgoing, dynamic.	Thrives on pressure, drive. Ready to challenge inertia, ineffectiveness, complacency and self-deception.	Prone to provocation, irritation and impatience.
Plant	The ideas person. Provides solutions.	Individualistic, serious-minded, unorthodox.	Imaginative, creative, solves difficult problems.	Too pre-occupied to communicate effectively. Disregards practical details, protocol.
Resource investigator	Explorer of opportunities. Good at developing outside contacts.	Enthusiastic, curious, communicative.	Capacity for contacting people. Explores opportunities. Ability to respond to challenge.	Liable to lose interest once the initial fascination has passed.
Monitor/ Evaluator	Analyser of options and good judge of things.	Sober, prudent.	Judgement, discretion, hard-headedness.	Lacks inspiration. Lacks ability to motivate others.
Team worker	The diplomat. Listens to all sides. Calms the waters.	Socially-oriented, perceptive, diplomatic.	Listens, builds, averts friction. Promotes team spirit.	Indecisiveness in crisis.
Completer	Looks after the detail, ensures nothing is missed.	Painstaking, orderly, conscientious.	Capacity to follow through. Perfectionism, delivers on time.	Can be a nit-picker. Reluctance to delegate. Inclined to worry unduly.

Team type	Team role	Typical features	Positive qualities	Allowable weaknesses
Specialist	Specialist in a particular subject area.	Single-minded, self-starting, dedicated.	Provides knowledge and skills in rare supply	Contributes only on a narrow front. Dwells on technicalities. Overlooks the 'big picture'.

Project Managers who know the natural roles of the team members can use that knowledge to build effective teams during the Starting Up a Project process for the management team and the Initiating a Project process when identifying team members. That knowledge can also be used to identify Project Managers.

Team types most suitable for Project Managers are typically shapers and implementers – those who want to get the job done, but in a controlled and planned way. According to Belbin the shaper is very much the 'let's get going' sort of person who is demanding of themselves and others. Shapers expect deadlines to be met, the work to be done and tend to challenge people and situations where they feel that the maximum is not being achieved. Outgoing and dynamic, the shaper is often found in managerial positions. A typical saying of the shaper might be 'Just do it'.

The implementer is concerned with turning concepts and plans into a practical working brief and carrying out that brief in a systematic fashion. The implementer has a knack for organisation and ensuring that the team's tasks have been properly structured and its objectives clearly defined. Implementers tend to be persevering people who will continue to struggle in the face of adversity to always achieve given objectives and deadlines. A typical implementer saying might be 'An ounce of action is worth a pound of theory'.

2.5 Getting off to a good start

When working in a group, getting off to a good start helps to establish the relationship between individual and team members that results in them being able to work together effectively. One theory of group dynamics (Tuckman and Jensen, 1997) suggests that groups go through a series of four phases, the first two involving conflict, the last two involving cohesion:

Forming	When the team first get together they start by discussing apparently unrelated issues, such as the weather or the traffic. During this time the individuals are trying to get to know each other and each one is trying to create an initial impression. This phase also establishes individual styles and authority. This may be a relatively short phase if the people already know each other.
Storming	This is the time of conflict and turbulence in the team's development. Individuals are

unsure about the purpose of the team, what they can contribute and what they can gain.

The group debates or even argues over the reasons for its existence, causing sub-groups with common interests to be formed and allowing natural leaders to emerge.

Norming	The norming phase sets a solid foundation for the performing phase. Team processes are established by consent and are followed.
Performing	This phase is actually only reached when all of the other phases have been completed. Here the team has reached maturity and it is using the process to work towards achieving the agreed goals. The objective of the Project Manager is to get the team to this point as quickly as possible and keep it there.

For a group in which the task is clearly defined and seen by all members as highly important, the first three stages may be dealt with in the first few hours of meeting. For most groups it takes longer and needs to be anticipated. Managers of project teams (involving people from different parts of the organisation) need to plan for and allow time for group development; less time should be needed when members come together from within one department.

During the forming stage the Project Manager should adopt a leadership style that focuses on tasks as opposed to relationships, concentrating on goals, standards, instruction, and getting acquainted experiences.

Conflict is natural and to be expected during the storming stage. Too much conflict creates chaos and too little conflict encourages apathy. Both are detrimental to team development. During this phase the Project Manager should focus attention on both the goal and on team members, encouraging active listening, assertiveness and clarification. In addition, attention should be given to being adaptable, flexible and creative while providing encouragement and support.

At the norming stage the Project Manager should be sharing the leadership functions and looking for a more participative role for the team members. Project Managers could also nurture member involvement by continuing the encouragement and support used during the previous stage.

At the performing stage, the Project Manager should be focusing on the risks, allowing moderate risks and being willing to accept modest failures. (Radical risk taking can destroy months of productive work when developing solutions). Focusing on keeping the communication channels open and rewarding project accomplishment is key to success during this stage.

There is one final phase called the mourning phase. This is often overlooked but is vitally important for two reasons. Firstly there is a lot of tidying up to do at the end of a project. This is the part that PRINCE2 handles exceptionally well with its controlled closure processes.

Secondly, as the formation of a performing team involved building relationships, both professional and personal, and significant amounts of energy and commitment, managing each person so that they can move on to the next team in a positive frame of mind is important.

2.6 Influencing skills

After discussing the various aspects of leadership theories and styles, it is clear that (unless you adopt an autocratic style as your only style) you will need to use influencing skills.

Influencing can be thought of as a four-stage process.

1   Gaining entry
    Successful influencing is often started by establishing contact on a personal level.
    Building trust and establishing both rapport and personal credibility are achieved
    in part by being aware of the situation and 'knowing your stuff'. You can achieve this
    through prior research including trying to understand the other person's expectations.

2   Joint diagnosis
    This involves a further understanding of each other's position. Questioning skills
    would come into play here. Relevant, open questions will help facilitate understanding of the other person's position, for example 'How do you feel about that?'
    or 'How does this proposal affect your area?'

    Confirmation of understanding can then be gained by the use of closed questions.
    For example 'So what you mean is…'. The deeper the understanding of the other
    person's position, the greater your ability to analyse it and make informed (and hence
    influential) comments. The matching of your position with the analysis of the other
    person's makes for the possibility of seeking and finding common ground. Focusing
    upon areas of common agreement early on in the process establishes a co-operative
    sense that enhances the possibility of agreement.

3   Effecting the change
    Active listening and verbal communication skills are fundamental to this. Even non-
    verbal communication is important in building the rapport necessary to achieve the
    objective. There will inevitably be differences of interest, and it is important to be able
    to negotiate (i.e. trade) where these occur. Although differences will occur, a good
    tactic is to build periodically on the common ground that you established at the start.

    Whenever making a suggestion, or trying to sell an idea, bear in mind the 'What's in it
    for me?' factor. Making proposals that only appear to have your interests at heart are
    unlikely to influence somebody to your point of view.

4   Consolidate
    It may be appropriate to conclude a successful encounter by clarifying what you have

agreed. If there are any actions, they must be carried out otherwise the impression that it was 'all talk' will be created, and attitudes may well revert. In other words it is important to be as good as your word. Checking back periodically may also be necessary, so that reinforcement can be given if required.

The advantages of this four-step approach to influencing are clear.

Being assertive in your personal approach will help you to be more influential. The calm, respecter of rights, who is not afraid to say 'no' in a polite and friendly manner is much more likely to be influential than someone who gets emotional or tries to bully.

Knowing your stuff, and showing that you are aware of the other person's position will 'get them on your side' quickly.

If you believe that the other person is wrong in their views, it can be dangerous to say so boldly. Tact and a clearly non-aggressive approach are more likely to win someone round, e.g. 'That's reasonable but have you considered…'.

Influencing is not about imposing solutions on people, it's about getting them to believe and accept that your views are the best answer for them.

2.7 Summary

There are many models of leadership and leadership style, team and group dynamics that have been developed over many years of research and investigation. These contrasting leadership approaches give an impression of how different styles may suit different situations within a project set-up.

Whilst each model on its own may not be applicable to every situation, the approach you adopt will need to be varied from situation to situation and from person to person to get the best progress or input from the individuals and the team.

Recognising the types of people you're dealing with – possibly with the aid of the Belbin model – may help determine and refine the leadership approach best suited to each. Different people respond to different types of stimuli. Initially it may be worth taking a middle line and adapting your style according to what you meet as the project progresses. There is a fine line to tread, however, between adapting to the situation's needs and being seen as inconsistent in your approach or, even worse, volatile.

3
PEOPLE, POLITICS AND THE PROJECT BOARD

3.1 Introduction

Key to the success of a project is the level of sponsorship and direction offered by the Project Board. Understanding the Project Board as a group, and the performance of the individuals fulfilling the Project Board roles, will identify how well-versed the Project Board is in directing a project.

Project Boards which have a good understanding of Management by Exception and Tolerance levels for time, cost, quality and scope, authority versus responsibility, the three-way partnership between business, users and specialists (especially where the specialist is an external supplier) should, from the Project Manager's view, be easier to work with. They will be likely to want to follow the 'event-driven' approach that is key to successful Project Boards.

Project Boards getting together for the first time may experience problems in letting go of the day-to-day control of the project or display a tendency towards the 'You're the Project Manager, you sort it out' approach. The degree to which the Project Manager is able to involve and draw support from the Project Board plays a large part in the smooth running of a project. To do this effectively, the Project Manager needs to be aware of how the foibles of individuals on the Project Board, and the politics within the Project Board and between it and the organisation, can come into play. Recognising what is at work and handling it appropriately are skills essential to the Project Manager.

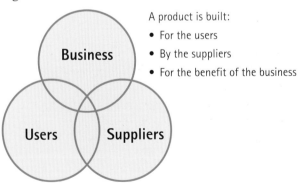

A product is built:
- For the users
- By the suppliers
- For the benefit of the business

Figure 3.1 The three-way partnership

The Project Manager may have managed projects many times before, but new Project Board members could be in uncharted waters, possibly feeling extremely vulnerable, all the more so

23

on business-critical projects. Project Managers need to be sensitive to this vulnerability and identify ways of making the board members more comfortable in their role, for example, by having time-driven, as opposed to event-driven, Project Board meetings or allowing more technically focused discussion to enable them to feel more at ease. The Project Manager also has to demonstrate that the project is under effective control. This may be at the temporary expense of some of the fundamental principles of the organisation component of PRINCE2. However, Project Managers should always be working to a strategy that ensures the Project Board adopts the principles in the longer term, whilst being aware of the risks that may be there in the transition period.

3.2 Typical people issues

There is huge scope to encounter people issues when dealing with the Project Board. In the previous chapter the underlying reasons for particular types of behaviour on projects was discussed. Making the correct choices of senior personnel is critical to the success of the project and overcomes the following common issues:

- It may be undecided who should undertake the role of Executive on the Project Board.

- If there is a choice of Project Managers for a project, what are the characteristics that can help identify the best one for a particular project?

- The selection criteria for appointing the remaining Project Board members may be unclear.

- Communications with a Project Board suffer the same difficulties of timing, content and frequency that are common to all organisations. The timing of communication with the Project Board and the wider organisation may be unclear, resulting in additional communication activities being put in place.

Before addressing the above people issues, the next section looks in more detail at typical personality traits that Project Managers may have to deal with.

3.3 Traits of Project Board members

Despite having defined roles and role definitions, Project Board members may well have characteristics and hidden agendas that could be damaging to the project and Project Manager.

The following draws together typical traits found in some Project Board members. There are two key points that should be remembered: first, that there are other traits and that some people can display either a combination or extremes of particular traits, and second, these traits can have positive aspects. For example, the strength of the natural leader in overcoming obstacles, and the precision of the micro-manager who ensures the finer points of the project are covered, etc. These positive aspects are not discussed here as it is the negative aspects that pose the most risk to the success of the project.

Table 3.1 Common traits found amongst Project Board members

Senior ditherers	**Example behaviour:** A senior manager who will not make a decision or will defer a decision until they see in which direction the rest of the group is going.
	Potential issues: This can be a significant problem if the ditherer is the Executive on the Project Board. The Project Manager will need to work hard to spell out choices and to present the favoured option clearly.
Natural leaders	**Example behaviour:** Natural leaders drive the project along; they make the ideal project champion and will move major obstacles out of the way of the Project Manager in order to get things done.
	Potential issues: The Project Manager must ensure that the natural leader does not ignore major issues and risks just because they may slow the project down.
Terrorists	**Example behaviour:** Terrorists come in several forms; the more extreme terrorist seems determined to wreck the project at every opportunity.
	Potential issues: Terrorists can be the type that do not want change, no matter what it is. They could also be under threat from the project, i.e. it could be a project that reduces their role, lowers their status in the organisation, reduces their team or even makes them redundant.
	Terrorism can also be generated by the perceived threat of being upstaged by the Project Manager, especially in a high profile project where the terrorist feels it should be them in the driving seat.
	One other type of terrorist may exist in other projects where a Project Manager or Project Board member may be aggrieved at having their resources and funding redirected to the new project.
Micro-managers	**Example behaviour:** This type of character is usually identified by phrases such as 'Show me in detail', 'I used to do this for a living, let me help you with the detail', 'I want to understand the underlying data here'.
	Potential issues: The Project Manager needs to be clear if there is a genuine nervousness with the information presented and therefore a need to increase the person's confidence in both the Project Manager and the information.
	This is significantly different to the senior manager who wants to get into the detail so that they can meddle. The validity and age of the experience, i.e. how up-to-date

Statesmen	**Example behaviour:** Statesmen, like terrorists, come in different forms. Some will use projects to achieve their own aims, either through the status of being on the Project Board and the ability to influence other members of senior management or by trying to influence the project's deliverables.
	Potential issues: Statesmen can be difficult and sometimes (from a project viewpoint) dangerous people to deal with. They are prone to changing their minds after making agreements; they can also remain squeaky clean whilst organising a mutiny.

a manager is in their understanding of the issues, is a key deciding factor in whether the Project Manager should allow this detailed study.

Developing strategies to cope with these potential issues can pose significant challenges for the Project Manager, especially if a mix of traits is displayed or the positive side of the trait needs to be covered.

The table below outlines some high-level points that could be considered when attempting to deal with these people.

Senior ditherers	Focus attention on needs as opposed to wants when asking for decisions. Focus on process and make the decision look routine. Limit the range of options that have to be picked when asking for a decision. Try to gain an understanding as to why decision-making is difficult. Use support of other managers to aid decision-making.
Natural leaders	Use risk management as a mechanism to demonstrate the impact of what can happen if an issue is not thought through. Ensure every impact analysis for every change is thorough.
Terrorists	Utilise support from project sponsor. Arrange a one-to-one meeting and ask for direct criticism about some of the issues.
Micro-managers	Utilise support from experts within the team in order to provide detail. Concentrate on the process used to gather information. Gain buy-in early.
Statesmen	Introduce formality. Keep detailed notes. Focus on the processes.

3.4 Appointing the Project Management team

The first three Starting Up a Project processes in a PRINCE2 project are all about designing and appointing the Project Management team, starting with the Executive, followed by the

26

Project Manager, then the rest of the team. Whilst this is clearly the best and recommended approach, there are other sequences of events that may occur, including a Project Manager appointing an Executive.

With due regard to the potential challenges presented by the types of characters mentioned above, awareness of them is often the only weapon, since their appointment may be a fait accompli.

3.4.1 The Executive

3.4.1.1 Identifying and appointing the Executive

There are typically three scenarios that determine the method of appointing the Executive:

- Self-appointment
  This will be the case if, for example, the project is part of a programme. In this situation the Project Mandate produced by the programme will specify whom this is to be – perhaps the programme manager or some other person in a programme management role.

  The self-appointment may also occur in situations where this project is a follow-on from a previous one. For example, the first project may have identified other products to be built and therefore the recommendation of the examining project issues process would have been to start a new project after the current one had finished.

- Incumbent in role
  For a project that has originated by another route (new strategy, market opportunity) then the Executive will most likely have been involved in securing funding for the project via the organisation's project approval process and will therefore already be in the role.

- Selection
  There may be situations where there is a Project Manager in place and based on their recommendation an Executive is suggested, then appointed. This may occur on projects that are being re-initiated or re-scoped. The original Executive may now no longer be the most appropriate person. In these cases the process described later for identifying and appointing other team members can be used to aid the decision-making process.

3.4.1.2 Characteristics of a good Executive

A good Executive for a Project Board would display three key characteristics:

- Authority
  The person should be senior enough within the organisation to make strategic decisions about the project (based on the Business Case). PRINCE2 is very clear about authority being consistent with accountability, hence 'senior enough'.

- Credibility
  It should be remembered that credibility within the organisation plays a significant part in the Executive's ability to lead and direct the project.

- Ability to delegate
  A key part of the Executive role is ensuring that the Project Manager is given enough 'space' to manage the project by keeping Project Board activity at the right level, i.e. directing a project. They should not be involved in the nitty-gritty of how the project is managed or in the specialist content of the project.

The Executive may require PRINCE2 support, perhaps from a Project Support Office or some other group that has PRINCE2 expertise and is aware of the responsibilities they are undertaking and the issues they will need to address.

3.4.2 The Project Manager

The assumption made throughout this book is that the reader is the Project Manager and has already been appointed as such on the project. But how did you become Project Manager and what criteria did the Executive use to identify and appoint you?

Assuming that the Executive is the first to be appointed (although, as stated earlier, this may not be the case), their first task is to find a suitable Project Manager. The Project Manager undertakes a significant proportion of the project management and therefore project management competencies rather than specialist expertise are a crucial requirement of the role.

Whilst some of the management theories previously mentioned can be used to identify the characteristics of a Project Manager, the project management role is so diverse in scope that a wide range of characteristics may 'fit'.

For example, Henry Mintzberg in his study of managerial work (1975) identified that managers, to a greater or lesser extent, have an interpersonal role, an informational role and a decisional role. Mintzberg sub-divided these further under each of these heading roles:

- Interpersonal roles
  - Leader
  - Liaison
  - Figurehead

- Informational roles
  - Monitor
  - Disseminator
  - Spokesperson

- Decisional roles
  - Entrepreneur
  - Disturbance handler
  - Resource allocator
  - Negotiator

Project Managers have to perform all of these roles on a daily basis. In addition, they have to be self-aware enough to know which role to step into at what time and for what 'audience'.

As well as identifying the characteristics and skills of the Project Manager, the Executive will need to balance the needs of the project, its risk to the organisation, the extent of change and the availability of internal resource.

There could be a case for employing an external Project Manager if the extent of change will be high. Bringing in an objective 'outsider' avoids cultural and/or personal attachments to the status quo. Also, an external Project Manager may be appropriate if a large part of the project is being contracted out to a third party whose Project Manager will perform the PRINCE2 Project Manager role and Team Manager role for that specialist group.

There should be a job specification for the Project Manager that the incumbent should sign. It is vitally important to ensure the role is clearly defined and is especially important when an external Project Manager is involved.

3.4.3 Other Project Board members

The process of identifying all the project interests, allocating these to appropriate Project Board roles, selecting people to undertake those roles and providing the Project Board with terms of reference may stem from previous work, a feasibility study for example.

If it is not clear who should perform these roles then a simple process can be followed to ensure that the most appropriate structure is put in place.

- Identify and describe project deliverables (from the Project Mandate)
- Identify all project interests
- Allocate interests to roles
- Prepare draft job descriptions

- Allocate named people to roles
- Appoint Project Board members and finalise job descriptions.

The Project Manager should recommend, in discussion with the Executive, the appropriate Project Management team for the project.

It is up to the Project Manager to design a suitable team structure, scaling it to the project size, risk and complexity. The board needs to represent all of the interested parties or stakeholders in the organisation (the users), and involve any suppliers (internal or external) that have been identified. (This is early in the project so it still might not be known who the stakeholders are or how they will be represented on the Project Board.)

There are a number of issues here about keeping the size of the Project Board as small as possible whilst still representing all business, user and supplier interests. A number of studies have demonstrated that smaller teams perform significantly better than larger ones. Weinberg (Brooks, 1995), in particular, demonstrated that communication channels between members of a team increase geometrically as the team size increases. Thus, with three people there are three communication channels, with four people there are six channels and with five people there are 10 channels and so on. (The mathematical formula for this is $(n^2 - n) \div 2$ where n is the number of people involved).

Producing a matrix of stakeholder against project products helps split the project stakeholders (who need to be part of the Communication Plan) from the project decision makers (who need to be on the Project Board).

In projects that impact on a large user community, some organisations have benefited from involving user groups. These groups discuss user issues and risks and pass recommendations to the Senior User on the Project Board. If a user group is involved, it is necessary to define at the outset who is authorised to represent its collective view and how this will operate.

The decision on whether to include external suppliers on the board may be a cultural one based on fear of divulging commercial or financial information. Leaving them out of the directing a project process could cause delays due to the lack of supplier resources to deal with change and to address major specialist/technical issues. It is the Executive's decision as to how this dilemma is solved practically.

Charles Handy (1993), a leading management thinker, identified that one of the key problems when working in large teams or complex environments is 'role ambiguity', knowing what your role is and how it fits with the rest of the team. Handy explained that in these large team environments roles often overlap, causing tension and confusion within the team. To avoid this, job descriptions should be produced which detail the duties required of each person who might potentially fulfil the various roles.

These may be based upon the role descriptions from the PRINCE2 manual, but tailored to suit the project. If there is a Project Support Office, they may hold template role definitions or job descriptions.

The role definitions/job descriptions should be competency-based, describing the suitable knowledge, experience and skills required, as well as the personal characteristics required. These can then be used to match the competencies of likely candidates that the Project Manager and Executive have identified.

This is done for a number of reasons:

- To confirm that candidates are suitable for the project
- To explain the project commitments
- To secure the candidate's agreement (by signature)
- To identify any support that the candidate may require to carry out their role successfully
- To identify the starting point for the candidate's induction to the project
- To decide how the Project Assurance role will be performed.

If there are political undercurrents at play in the appointment of an individual this will become apparent when using this approach. Appropriate action can be taken to ensure that, whilst the appointment may be required, the Project Board does not suffer as a result of lack of competency in a particular area.

The Project Board's first challenge is to knit together and perform as a team. This may require some facilitation and support as it goes through the cycle of forming, storming, norming and performing (see Section 2.5 for a definition of these terms). The tailored job descriptions and the directing a project process framework will help with the norming stage of the cycle. The aim is to move through all the directing a project lower level processes with a minimum of conflict.

3.4.4 Briefing the Project Board and gaining approval

Once Project Board members are formally appointed, a briefing has to take place to elaborate on their roles and on the project and gain their agreement for beginning their education process. This could take the form of workshops, discussions or training courses. The Project Manager, the Executive, the Programme or Project Support Office or some external experts could carry out the facilitation of these courses. Even if the Project Board is familiar with PRINCE2 roles and processes this may still be necessary to ensure consistent communication.

The Project Manager needs to ensure that all the Project Board members are briefed on the progress of the management products, i.e. the Project Brief and initiation Stage Plan, via informal briefings before the final Project Board meeting at the end of the Starting Up a Project process.

This will ensure that the Project Board is familiar with the content of the products they are approving, even if they have not seen them in their final form.

3.4.5 Communication with the rest of the organisation

Without a good communication process in place the stakeholders not included on the Project Board could be resentful at their exclusion. There may be others who are suspicious of the project goals or fearful of the project outcomes.

To calm these fears, and mitigate any such negativity and the risk it represents, the Project Board needs to communicate outside of the project as early as the Starting Up a Project process.

The Project Board needs to inform other parts of the organisation that the project is about to get underway (at the start of Initiating a Project) and that contributions may be required such as access to a Project or Programme Support Office. Communicating the planning for project resources and accommodation will make the extent of the project needs known.

Communications should be based upon the approved Project Brief, Project Approach and plan for the initiation stage. They are therefore likely to be approved for circulation at the first meeting of the Project Board.

Hints and tips – Who should serve on a Project Board?

Who should be selected to undertake the roles on a PRINCE2 Project Board? Selection should be based on the following criteria:

- seniority
- authority
- project priority
- availability
- knowledge
- experience.

Project Board members should be of appropriate seniority and possess the requisite authority to take the decisions needed. Seniority and authority must be matched to the project's size, strategic importance and degree of risk. Although PRINCE2 limits the formal involvement of the Project Board to specific control meetings (e.g. end stage assessments), Project Board members should be available to give the time and attention needed by the project throughout its life.

There is often a balance to be struck between seniority and availability. There is no point in appointing someone to a Project Board if they are seldom available when required. Likewise having someone available but with no authority or seniority would be just as pointless.

This point has been identified in many studies, most notably in the UK Government's review of major IT projects, *Successful IT: Modernising government in action*, also known as the McCartney Report (2001). One of the many recommendations in the report is to 'aim to encourage good leadership and establish clear responsibility for IT-based change programmes and projects'. To achieve this projects need to have a Senior Responsible Owner with a detailed description of the responsibilities of the role. This role matches that of Project Board Executive.

The question of project priority is also important when considering Project Board members. This should be defined in the Project Brief and senior management should make clear the relative priorities of project and line management duties.

This priority applies to other team members as well. There is a constant need to reconcile project needs and line commitments, project activities and 'business as usual'. This applies to all levels of a project organisation where the people fulfilling the various roles are not involved full-time on the project. It is an unfortunate reality that urgent issues regarding the day job must often take priority over project needs.

The knowledge and experience required of Project Board members should include PRINCE2 and project management as well as competence in the relevant functional area. It is sometimes not recognised by Project Board members that they need to understand their PRINCE2 roles although they can occasionally be too senior to be told so! Setting standards, in terms of training or experience needed by each of the PRINCE2 organisation roles, can be of help here.

The appropriate background for the Executive role sometimes causes difficulty. The role of the Executive is to represent senior management, business and financial interests. The upper echelons of the finance function are often regarded as the appropriate source of the Executive role although other senior managers can undertake it. This should be the case if one thinks of the owner/user of the business product as the person with the most to lose if the project fails, i.e. 'the buck stops with them'.

It should be remembered that it is possible to combine the senior management, finance and business interests in one person, especially if, for example, the business and financial interests are in conflict. These are matters of principle to be resolved outside the project.

3.5 Project Board meetings

3.5.1 Introduction

PRINCE2 says that there are five types of events that would cause a Project Board to meet:

- authorising initiation
- authorising a project
- authorising a stage
- authorising an exception plan
- confirming project closure.

This section describes how to get the best out of Project Board meetings and avoid any issues of conflict within the management team.

3.5.2 Preparation

It is assumed that the Project Manager is familiar with the logistics of preparing a meeting. Preparation for any type of Project Board meeting needs to cover the following areas:

- preparing the management products for approval and sign-off (see Section 3.5.2.1)
- preparing information for any decisions that are required
- working with the Executive to structure the meeting and produce the agenda
- briefing the Project Board Executive.

3.5.2.1 Preparing the products for approval and sign-off

The preparation of products for approval covers the following:

- the Product Initiation Document (or any PID sections that have been revised)

- the next Stage Plan
- exception plan
- the project closure products (Follow-on Actions, Lessons Learned Report, etc.).

As stated earlier in this section, all of the above should have been discussed with the Project Board members prior to the meeting. This may be the first time they have seen the complete product, therefore products should be distributed in advance.

3.5.2.2 Structuring the meeting

The relationship between the Senior Supplier(s) and Senior User(s) has an influence on the agenda and structure of the meeting.

If, for example, the Project Board is constructed such that the Executive and Senior User are from the customer organisation and suppliers are external, this may lead to a split Project Board meeting.

The first part of the meeting could be for discussing sensitive issues such as the Business Case, end user issues and supplier performance with only the Executive and Senior User. Once issues and discussions have been resolved, completed or actioned, the supplier organisation can then join the meeting.

In a project where there are multiple users, for example in a project implementing a product across the whole of an organisation, there may be a user committee. One member of this committee would represent the whole committee on the Project Board.

This may also be true of suppliers, especially where several suppliers are working on the delivery of one product, for example in a large office move, where suppliers installing desks may be working in conjunction with a different supplier who is fitting the flooring. In this example the various supplier departments and external suppliers may have a separate committee and again be represented on the Project Board by one of their members. However this may be better formalised as a supplier and sub-contractor relationship.

In this scenario it is essential that the various groups have met and ratified all outstanding issues with the products being presented for approval.

For new Project Boards the early Project Board meetings (authorising initiation and authorising a project) although not mandatory, should be held and include an education element covering the important aspects of the project processes. The Project Manager should guide the project processes and confirm that they have been understood.

3.5.2.3 Producing the agenda

Despite the fact that Project Board meetings are chaired and run by the Executive, as Project Manager you will still be involved in the arranging of the meeting, including producing and distributing the agenda.

The Executive should agree the agenda and the structure of the meeting before the agenda is published.

The basic reason for an agenda is that if there is no defined objective for a meeting there is a good chance the meeting may run into trouble. There are many things that will happen at Project Board meetings. They provide opportunities to:

- inform – when a formal presentation is not appropriate
- make decisions – probably following some debate
- get agreement – by airing and resolving difficulties
- gather information – by seeking the collective wisdom of a number of people
- review progress – using the End Stage Report or (if potential problems have been identified) the Highlight Reports produced during the previous stage
- build the team – by encouraging communication, recognising achievement and discussing problems
- let off steam – by discussing an emotive issue with the object of clearing the air.

As the Project Board does not meet that often, the meetings are as much about developing trust, building an *esprit de corp*, and strengthening teamwork and communication between the attendees as about disseminating information.

Of course, meetings may arise for a combination of reasons; the important thing is that the objectives of the meeting are clear in people's minds.

The objectives of the meeting should be decided and expressed on the agenda. Having set the objectives, the topics and the length of time to be spent on each one should be defined.

The agenda items should be ordered so that simple and quick items are covered first, leaving time for the longer discussions later.

As a general principle, meetings tend to become less productive the longer they are. Most people become restless and lose concentration after about two hours. If it is absolutely necessary to have a long meeting, then a break after two hours should be called, and every hour or so after that. This should be reflected in the agenda.

The topics to be discussed should now be formalised into an agenda and sent out to all attendees. This should be done in good time to allow everyone time to prepare.

3.5.2.4 Briefing the Executive

This is one of the most important jobs the Project Manager has to do. Getting this right at the early stages of the project will enable you to:

- generate a level of trust and confidence in the Executive that you are the right person for the job and you know what you are doing

- develop an open and honest relationship to such an extent that if you need to call on the Executive at short notice in the future you will gain priority access

- be given a hearing when making suggestions.

The briefing meeting, like the Project Board meeting, should be planned and thought through to ensure that the best can be made of the short time available from a busy senior manager. Every aspect of the Project Board agenda should be discussed, as should potential problems that may arise as a result. These may include issues of viability, risk and scope as well as any people problems.

During the meeting it is vital to remember that the Executive may be in a position where they are feeling vulnerable. They may have never been in the position of leading a Project Board before; they may be managing a business-critical multi-million pound project. You, on the other hand, as a PRINCE2 practitioner, understand the process and procedures involved in managing a project. You should 'talk up' at all times, making the assumption that they understand the subject you are discussing without over-explaining or omitting crucial details simply because they are complicated.

People do not like to be patronised. If the discussion is 'over their head' they should let you know they are being left behind. Early in the relationship you may have to use other skills to check understanding. Look for body language clues that may suggest confusion or lack of understanding. Later, when the relationship has matured, you will get to know their strengths and weaknesses and be able to adjust your conversational style to suit.

Hints and tips – The Project Board meeting

There are many excellent books that discuss meetings and how to run them (Blanchard, 1995, 2000; Hodgson, 1993; McCormack, 1996; Video Arts, 1991). Rather than replicate all of the good work documented in those books, this section focuses on some specific points that apply particularly to Project Board meetings:

- who's in charge?

- discussion and decision

- follow-up and follow through.

Who's in charge?

As a Project Manager you have to keep in mind that this is a Project Board meeting. The Project Manager is not a member of the Project Board, you are an invited guest.

Whilst you may have experience and knowledge on your side, you are not in charge. Having spent time briefing the Executive you should sit back and let them control the meeting in their own style. Project Managers should not dominate the meeting and should offer opinions only when asked to do so.

'Knowing your place' may appear to be an old-fashioned view of how to behave in a meeting. However, this is a meeting of senior management discussing their project and the viability of their project. Your role is to provide the facts in a professional and assertive manner, allowing them to make the appropriate decision as to whether or not the project should proceed to the next stage.

Discussion and decision

One of the frequent problems experienced by Project Board meetings is the failure to recognise the difference between discussion and decision.

If there is no decision on a topic, any minutes taken need to reflect the discussion that has taken place and the activities that need to happen in order for a decision to be made.

If a decision is made at the Project Board meeting the minutes should reflect only the actual decision, not the activity leading up to the decision.

When a decision or action is documented, the Project Manager needs to ensure that all decisions fit the SMART criteria and are:

- **S**pecific
- **M**easurable
- **A**chievable
- **R**ealistic
- **T**imely.

In the book *McCormack on Communicating* (1996) Mark McCormack gives some examples of instructions that have very little meaning:

- 'This document needs more focus'
- 'Make it go away'
- 'Just do it'

- 'Get a better handle on this'
- 'This needs more work'
- 'Figure it out and get back to me'
- 'Breathe some life into this project'
- 'I'm not convinced, convince me'.

These are comments we either use or see in writing many times in our working lives. Taking the first comment ('This document needs more focus') as an example, and applying the SMART rules, highlights the following questions:

- Specific – Which aspects of the document needs more focus, all of it or just one section?
- Measurable – How will I know when I have a focused document?
- Achievable – How do I make the document focused and who is going to provide the detail to do this?
- Realistic – Can this actually be done and, if it can, is it sensible to do so?
- Timely – When does this need to be done and how much effort should we put into it?

A Project Board meeting is not a democracy, i.e. the Executive's decision is final. It is important, however, that there is enough discussion to enable the Executive to focus on clarifying decisions or recognising what other work has to be done. Always remember that PRINCE2 has an excellent tool for dealing with this issue – the Product Description.

Minutes detailing discussion or decisions should follow the CABS principle:

- **C**lear
- **A**ccurate
- **B**rief
- **S**tructured

Follow-up and follow through

The minutes of the Project Board meeting should be produced as soon as possible after the meeting, ideally within 24 hours. As the Project Manager you should follow up every decision and action item documented in the minutes. The Daily Log can be helpful in scheduling follow-up actions. Following up the action, however, is not the same as following every action through to its conclusion. This could span several project stages.

The Project Manager needs to ensure that momentum is maintained and that progress is fed back to the Project Board via the Highlight Report process as a minimum. An alternative is to document the action item as a project issue and use the project's Issue Log to ensure that the required focus is maintained on resolving the action items.

3.6 Summary

The role of the Project Board on a PRINCE2 project is crucial to the project's success. The quality of the input from the Project Board also impacts on the smooth running of a project and it is the Project Manager's responsibility to elicit that input in the right way and at the right time.

This means understanding the personalities involved, their personal and political agendas and steering a course to ensure project interests are at the forefront of everyone's minds and actions when they need to be.

To bring this about, the Project Manager has not just to be competent but has to come across as both competent and assertive with the Project Board. A sound awareness and understanding of the broad context of the project should illuminate some of the issues Project Board members may face, and help to predict issues and provide the key to their resolution.

It is in the Project Manager's interests to keep on top of communication issues with the Project Board so that their contribution is kept at the optimum level, i.e. enough involvement to maintain progress but not so much that they (or the Project Manager) view it as handholding or a burden.

A Project Manager should therefore try to identify and understand what may be in the minds of the various Project Board members and demonstrate astuteness and assertiveness in understanding how those things may surface in the project and how to handle them appropriately when they do.

4
PLANNING AND ESTIMATING

This section describes the people-related activities, events and issues that need to be addressed in order to plan and execute a project effectively, and ensure that there is appropriate involvement of user and specialist resources. It is the people aspects, i.e. their unpredictability, that make planning both very necessary and rather difficult.

4.1 Planning

Planning is a craft, a mixture of science (logical steps and techniques which aid the creations of plans) and art (estimating). It is the level of confidence (or lack of it) that needs to be understood by all project members (including the Project Manager) involved in the planning process. An estimated completion date is a guess, a 'best guess' based on a number of documented assumptions and information, but still a guess.

Therefore the Project Board should not expect, nor should the Project Manager provide, a 100% confidently predicted end date if the Project Board's expectations are to be managed effectively. Rather, the Project Manager should be able to say that with the information they have they are, for instance, '60% confident that a project can be delivered within a six to seven month window'. As the project progresses, at the end of every stage, it should be possible to increase the level of confidence and narrow the range of completion dates. However they can only be 100% confident about completion dates and costs when the project product has been delivered. The core of this chapter looks at how to determine these levels of confidence, what factors to build into planning and estimating and what techniques can improve the accuracy of planning.

4.1.1 Typical people issues

There are different responses to planning – often based on the Project Manager's personality type. 'Doers' like to act; 'thinkers' prefer to plan. Both activities are required since 'planning without action is sterility; action without planning is chaos'.

Many excuses are made for not planning, including dealing with views such as 'the project has to get going' or that 'this type of project has been done before so planning is not necessary'. A team's failure to plan can be due to them never having been taught how to do it properly. It is important to be clear on:

- who should be involved in the planning process
- how estimates are produced
- how one determines the right amount of Tolerance.

4.1.2 Interpreting the planning processes

There is no mystique to planning. It is concerned with identifying:

- What is going to be produced
- Who is needed in order to produce it
- What is needed in order to produce it
- When it can be produced
- How long it is going to take
- How much it is going to cost.

It is essential to strike a balance between doing sufficient planning to get underway and getting into analysis (or planning) paralysis. In the words of John Lennon, 'Life is what happens to you while you're busy making other plans'. The use of different Levels of Plans (Project, Stage and Team) will help with the dilemma of having to plan into the future when you know that people will:

- go sick
- leave
- overestimate
- underestimate
- be lazy (McGregor's theory X worker)
- lie about progress and achievements
- forget to do what they are told to do (or worse, do what they want to do despite having been told not to).

4.1.3 What to plan and who/where to get estimates from

To overcome the difficulty in planning the future in detail, PRINCE2 offers plans at different levels and advocates a product-based approach to planning.

The Product Breakdown Structure is helpful in getting down to a level of product at which people can understand, plan for and control their delivery. The Product Descriptions then clarify each product at this level and help with planning by defining, amongst other things:

- what the product contains (the composition)

- what is available to contribute to its production (the derivation)

- how demanding to be about checking that the product is fit for the purpose (quality criteria and checking method).

This allows you to both communicate expectations to the team, that is what they have to do and by when, and plan for the review and sign-off activities.

4.2 Estimating

The appropriate people to involve in the planning process are those who have experience of the project's business, specialist and user environments. This means the Project Board (or its delegated representatives – Project Assurance), Team Managers and members of project teams who are specialists in their field. Clear responsibilities will help in the process. The Project Manager is responsible for producing Project and Stage Plans. Project Support assists in the process providing specialist skills in the use of, for example, planning tools and estimating techniques. The next section outlines four generic estimating techniques that can be used by both the Project Manager and Project Support.

4.2.1 Generic estimating techniques

4.2.1.1 Expert judgement

The expert judgement technique is also known as the Delphi method because of the oracle at Delphi in Greek mythology. There will certainly be variations, but the main features of the technique are to:

- put a group of experts into a room

- pose the question, e.g. how long will it take to produce this feasibility study report?

- allow discussion to clarify the question

- obtain estimates (secret ballots help to reduce the problems of peer pressure here)

- let the estimates be seen and get justification for any outside the norm (some people may have specialist knowledge unavailable to the others)

- allow people to change their minds

- go through a number of iterations if required

- calculate the average.

The technique has advantages and disadvantages. It is a good way of pooling expertise, but it is prone to error if the wrong people are involved. Also, people may privately revise their good estimates so as not to appear silly in the light of other people's offerings. This peer pressure can distort people's judgement.

Overall though, in a situation where expert judgement is sought, use of a formal technique such as the Delphi method introduces discipline into a situation where it might not otherwise be present.

4.2.1.2 Analogy

Arguably the best technique for estimating anything is to have information on previous experiences in the same area. The Analogy technique is based upon analysing actual effort used on previously completed projects and comparing those earlier projects with those currently being estimated.

Historical information is an extremely valuable basis for future estimating, but it is dependent on the information having been recorded accurately. It clearly takes time to amass and requires recording in some useable format, but many organisations have found that the investment of effort has more than paid for itself in improved estimating.

The simplest method of recording the information is in the form of the original Project and Stage Plans, marked up with actuals. To be useful, these really should be accompanied by some form of narrative, perhaps in the Daily Log. This would explain and record the reasons for any early or late completion of products against the original estimates, thus allowing realistic interpretation of the situation at the time. This information may be held in any company-wide Project Support Office, so you should investigate what they can offer your project, both in the provision of information and process support.

4.2.1.3 Top down

Top down estimating is concerned with estimating for the whole project and is conducted at a high level.

The Product Flow Diagram is used to identify the major stages in the project, based upon product delivery and major decision points.

Initial estimates are produced for the products in each stage and the estimates for each stage are combined to provide an overall estimate.

This technique is ideally used at the feasibility study (where one is conducted), then at project initiation to refine those estimates and again at the end of each stage of the project, with the estimates becoming more and more accurate as the project proceeds.

4.2.1.4 Bottom up

Bottom up estimating is carried out at stage planning time, when a clear idea of the products and their nature (via Product Descriptions) is known.

The idea behind Bottom up estimating is a simple one. It relies upon the fact that a small and simple activity is easier to estimate than a large and complex one, but that large and complex is only several small and simple elements considered together.

4.2.2 Use of techniques

These techniques can be used together at various points in the project life cycle. One estimating technique is not necessarily better than another. The best way to estimate is to use a combination of the techniques at various points in the project life cycle, applying them through planning workshops at the various stage end points.

The planning workshops at the beginning of a project serve many purposes, not least to build team spirit and ownership in the resulting plan. In order to produce a reasonable estimate for a project the Project Manager may wish to clarify the following at the planning workshop:

- Do all attendees understand what is required?
- Are they familiar with the type of work?
- What other work do they have?
- What is their availability?
- Are they objective and reliable?

Obtaining estimates requires some people management skills. If asking people to estimate on their own, check they understand what the estimate is for and go through it with them in detail if necessary.

- Do they have knowledge of the type of product you want an estimate for? Could they produce an estimate anyway, even perhaps with lower accuracy? If not, whom should you be asking?
- Do they have the time to produce the estimate, and does the time required relate to effort or elapsed time?
- Are they available to carry out the work?
- Have they been objective when preparing the estimate and are they reliable?
- Will they carry out the work as estimated?
- Is the estimate worthwhile?

The estimator must remember the need to allow for normal staff commitments (holiday, training, interviews, etc.) and for social interaction (tea, chat, etc.). The estimator should only allow between three and four days per week productive time.

If in doubt, you must query aspects of the estimate in order to gain confidence.

Perhaps the Project Board, or a member of it, does not agree with your estimates for a project. However, if they have been prepared on a sound basis and have been reviewed by a third party, you are in a strong position to carry the day since any discussion on constraints or deadlines can be backed up by hard evidence.

The use of estimate planning sheets and Product Descriptions will greatly ease the production of estimates and any subsequent discussions. Planning sheets merely record the assumptions made in arriving at the estimate for the task or product, the estimating methods used and the reasons for any amendment to the estimates. They can be a useful means of re-estimating at later stages and contribute to lessons learned messages about planning.

4.2.3 Team size and effects on estimates

We intuitively know that although putting more people onto a task will reduce its duration, it is not as simple as doubling the resources and halving the time. This is because as the number of people on a task rises there are more opportunities for communication and control problems to slow down the work. What makes it worse is that sometimes it is only practical for one person to work on a particular task. Therefore as team size goes up, the efficiency of the individuals in the group actually goes down. This phenomenon is known as Weinberg's Rule, a rule of thumb that states if you triple the team size, you will only double its productivity (Brooks, 1995).

Estimates should reflect this as well as the skills and actual productivity of people in order to arrive at realistic plans.

Hints and tips for making the planning and estimating processes work effectively

- Choose the appropriate estimating technique for the project based on knowledge of the project, your organisation and the available information to support the planning process.

- Use estimating sheets to record some of the detailed assumptions made when estimating.

- Avoid duplication of 'contingency' – adding extras during the estimating process and then again when analysing risks means the timescales and costs are over-inflated and the project Business Case may not be viable.

- Get the right people involved – people who are subject matter experts (suppliers and users) and people who understand the process of planning and estimating. These could be Team Managers or from the Project Board, Project Assurance or Project Support.

- Be objective, realistic (not pessimistic) and honest about the estimates produced.

4.2.4 Risks

As noted above, it can be expected that a calculated amount of 'contingency' time is included in the estimating since there are foreseeable risks and unforeseeable events (accidents and errors) to be allowed for. Among the types of risk to be managed within a project or host organisation (political, environmental, technical) the unpredictability and vulnerability of the people constitutes a significant area.

Some people do not like to consider risks. There is a commonly expressed view that this is seen as too negative or pessimistic. It is, however, pragmatic and professional to plan to avoid or counteract those future events that might impact your project or the Business Case objectives. Some of the risks to be faced are:

- role overload – having too much to do
- role underload – not having enough to do
- personality clashes
- team members getting on too well – too much socialising, covering for each other's mistakes, etc.
- role conflicts (with other roles or overlaps in responsibility)
- motivation
- uncontrolled enthusiasm – team members all with good ideas, each doing their own thing with no central co-ordination.

Some risks will be identified by the make-up of the project team itself. Personality clashes and a mismatch of team roles or personality types may cause communication breakdowns and delays. Planning for the selection and induction of people so they are productive as quickly as possible, and feel their contribution is valued, may alleviate this. It will avoid demoralisation, confusion, lack of understanding or desertion of the people you need for the success of the project.

PRINCE2 advocates risk analysis and management in planning, as there is a natural tendency to be over-optimistic in planning even if estimating for other people. Risk analysis then brings a realistic (but not pessimistic) assessment to bear on estimates and other aspects of the plan.

4.3 Dealing with resource conflicts

During the planning process you will inevitably discover that the resources available do not match the needs of the project. It is your responsibility to manage the project activities to deliver against the Project Brief but only if the Project Board provides resources with both the skill and availability to complete the work.

The first step in resolving this issue is to look at the plan and identify if there is any spare time between the finish of one product and the start of the next (commonly referred to as 'float'). The second step is to look at the task dependencies to see if they can be altered. If neither of these options resolves the problem then you will need to escalate the matter to the Project Board and present them with practical and costed options and a recommendation. This will require some analysis, research and evidence of the issue. Presenting the Project Board with a Gantt chart and resource histogram will demonstrate the problem but it may also serve to inspire their confidence in the process you have used to generate these products. Involving Project Assurance from the outset should allay some of their questions.

Alternatives could be explored, such as:

- sharing resources with operational departments
- bringing in external consultants
- doing deals with other projects.

In the final analysis the Project Board is in the best position to be aware of the 'bigger picture' and take a business-based decision about the priorities within the project. If it cannot all be completed with the resources available the options are:

- Do less. Reducing the scope allows more time and money to complete the remaining work but delivers less.

- Do it later. Increasing the timescale creates a larger window in which to complete the work but it will cost more and may miss critical deadlines.

- Do it less well. Reducing the quality is a favourite of many projects as it effectively de-scopes the project without reducing functionality. Cutting corners now, however, can store problems for later on. For example, saving time by not delivering any documentation may make the product insupportable in the future.

- Add more resources. Throwing more people at the task may seem a good idea, but it should be borne in mind that increasing team size does not necessarily increase productivity by the same proportion.

If a resource conflicts exists between projects, then the Project Board should decide which project is more important to the organisation as a whole.

4.4 Briefing the Project Board and gaining approval

The other aspect of completing the plan includes adding the final text of the plan (prerequisites, assumptions, plan descriptions, etc.) as well as discussing the plan with the Project Board. It is not just at the end of the planning process that the Project Board needs to be briefed. The members should also be briefed on how the planning process will work – the steps in the process – and how and when the Project Board will be involved. Finally the Project Board should decide whether any Project Assurance processes should be delegated, and to whom, and the Project Manager's involvement in that process. All of the above will facilitate the Project Board signing off the plan as a suitable control tool for its project.

4.5 Summary

Project Managers have to deal with many of the excuses made for not planning projects sufficiently (e.g. 'the project needs to get going' or 'this type of project has been done before so planning is not necessary').

One of the key aspects of planning is to generate a level of confidence, which needs to be understood and communicated to all project team and Project Board members involved in the planning process. This level of confidence should be able to demonstrate that the project was estimated correctly.

The appropriate people to involve in the planning process are those who have experience of the project's business, specialist and user environments. Project Support assists in the process providing specialist skills in the use of, for example, planning tools and estimating techniques.

In order to produce a reasonable estimate for a project the Project Manager may wish to consider planning workshops at the beginning of a project as they serve many purposes, not least to build team spirit and build ownership in the resulting plan.

During the planning process risks will be identified and, as there is a natural tendency to be over-optimistic in planning, PRINCE2 advocates risk analysis and management as a discrete process.

During the planning process you will inevitably discover that the resources available do not match the needs of the project. Your responsibility to manage the project activities to deliver against the Project Brief can only be discharged effectively if the Project Board provides people with both the skill and availability to complete the work.

In the final analysis the Project Board is in the best position to be aware of the 'bigger picture' and take a business-based decision about the priorities within the project.

It is important therefore that the Project Board members are briefed on progress during the planning process, as this will facilitate the Project Board signing off the plan.

5

BUILDING PROJECT TEAMS

This section describes the people activities, events and issues associated with the delivery of projects.

From a people perspective, there are some fundamental things the Project Manager needs to put in place such as: the project team, the management processes that the team will follow to ensure quality and monitor and report progress and the relationship with any third-party suppliers.

Having these fundamentals in place, the Project Manager then needs to manage and lead the team, manage the Project Board and any political issues that may exist and deal with any problems that arise.

5.1 Typical people issues

Apart from defining the scope, quality, and reporting requirements in Work Packages, PRINCE2 does not and cannot (as it is a management method as opposed to a technical method) resolve the issues surrounding the project team. The Project Manager may have to overcome some problems arising directly from the people issues:

- Selecting the project team
  - Free choice versus no choice. Some project teams are inherited, others the Project Manager can choose and others again may be a mix of both.
  - How does the Project Manager ensure they have the right people to get the job done?
  - If you do not have the right people what can you do about it?
  - How does the PRINCE2 Work Package help prevent people issues arising?

- Monitoring performance
  - The Project Plan is based on estimates. How, therefore, can the team's performance be monitored in order to ensure the estimates are being achieved?

- Difficult team members
  - What is the difference between discipline and misconduct and is there a way of dealing with both effectively?

5.2 Building the project team

Building the project team is not a simple process, even if the team is already in place. As Project Manager, a significant amount of work has to be done to identify the best people for each of the tasks and to identify any potential skills gaps, especially if there are no Team Managers in place.

The first steps towards this are the selection and induction procedures. It should be remembered that even if you have no choice in the selection of people on your team, it might still be worthwhile going through an interview process. This can pinpoint at the earliest any gaps in the person's skills, knowledge and experience, and could lead to further training, additional risk management on planned activities and changes to estimates.

5.2.1 Selection

Project team selection may be a Project Manager's first experience of recruitment from the 'other side of the desk'. Whilst everyone has presumably experienced selection from the point of view of being a candidate, this does not imply they will be comfortable or competent in the role of interviewer. For that reason, the next sub-sections describe how a Project Manager could approach that new challenge.

The Stage Plans should identify the skills required in the project team(s). The problem at this stage lies in matching real people and their real skills against the ideal skill-set required to do the work. An exact match is rare and the process has to be carried out in a systematic way establishing where people need support to carry out their assigned roles.

One way of assessing people is to use competency profiles as a common benchmark. This can assist in the selection and recruitment process and also identify training needs for the induction.

For each role, personal and specialist competencies should be identified. Personal competencies are qualitative and will focus on 'fit with the team'. Specialist competencies can usually be quantified using the KES schema described in Figure 5.1.

Knowledge

- Know about a subject (what)
- Understand a subject (why)
- Theoretical (via training, books, etc.)

Experience

- Can apply knowledge (how)
- Has used theory
- Usually stated in period of time (e.g. 6 months)

Skill

- Can demonstrate a stated level of ability
- Measurable via quality criteria

Figure 5.1 KES schema on specialist competencies

The competencies required to carry out each of the major tasks of a job can be identified and classified as:

- a knowledge requirement (knowledge and awareness about a subject, the what and why)

- an experience requirement (applying the knowledge in practice, often expressed in periods of time)

- a skill requirement (ability to practise the requirement to a defined and measurable level).

Thus, a job might require knowledge of a subject alone or an amount of knowledge and experience, or an amount of knowledge, experience and a defined level of skill. This can be illustrated using project planning as an example.

A Project Board member would be expected to have knowledge of project planning (what and why) but not necessarily to be experienced in it. A PRINCE2 Project Manager would expect to be knowledgeable, experienced and skilled.

It is very important to make this distinction when analysing jobs and tasks, otherwise a great degree of confusion and misinterpretation of job requirements can be made. For example, does an IT Project Manager require IT technical knowledge, knowledge and experience or knowledge, experience and skill?

Once potential candidates (internal as well as external to the organisation) are selected from applications or CVs, they can be interviewed against the same profile, encouraging a fair selection process. This is especially important in the climate of non-discriminatory selection. It is advisable to retain records of why people were not selected for a post both for the sake of good record-keeping and in case of employment tribunals.

The interview itself ought to be structured around three distinct phases:

- the introduction
- the in-depth interview
- the conclusion.

5.2.1.1 The introduction

This phase should achieve the objectives of relaxing the candidate (and the interviewer) and enabling the interviewer to take control. This is best achieved by a warm smiling face followed by a firm handshake and an outline of the objectives, structure and planned duration of the interview (taken from the previously prepared interview plan based on the candidate's CV). Austerity achieves nothing, apart from potentially unsettling candidates and perhaps putting them off the job. The introduction is also the time when the role and its implications for competencies development should be discussed and 'sold'.

5.2.1.2 The in-depth interview

The first guideline to in-depth interviewing is to stick to the interview plan and avoid being led off the subject by intriguing but irrelevant answers to questions. Keeping to the topic area enables control to be maintained and details to be probed and examined. It is vital to take notes so that these can be analysed later.

When interviewing individually, taking notes can be a difficult operation that can easily affect the quality of interviewing in an adverse way. Using more technically sophisticated methods of recording interviews, e.g. tape recorders, video cameras, etc., is still too disconcerting to be practical. An effective method can be to take a deliberate break between topics to document the evidence separately. This gives the candidate a rest and enables the interviewer to concentrate on active listening and follow-up questioning without the concern of simultaneous recording.

An interviewer must be an active listener. This is not as easy as it sounds. There are two aspects to listening. Not only is it important to absorb what is being said, but also to show that you are listening. When someone is talking they are aware of the signals you are giving, such as nodding or saying 'mmm' and giving other signs of interest.

Feedback from the previous question is also a listening signal. The use of words like 'what' and 'how' ('What effect did that have?' and 'How did that work?') are indicative of this.

When confronted by a silent interviewer with an enigmatic stare or constantly cast down eyes, the speaker may become withdrawn or aggressive, thus detracting from the fact-finding process.

The interviewer must listen for a number of reasons. It is necessary to listen first to what is being said in an attempt to evaluate the candidate's words. Listening intelligently allows the interviewer to pick up 'feeds', i.e. indications of further knowledge.

This is where the interview can resolve any discrepancy between what people claim they can do, and have done, compared with reality. A person appointed on a spurious claim who is then unable to deliver presents a risk to the project. Investigation of these claims by probing with further and deeper questioning identifies the facts which otherwise might be obscured behind generalities. A candidate may say: 'I have undertaken an external course of study in…'. This may indicate an ambitious, hard working individual, but the interviewer cannot be satisfied with an unsupported assertion. Was the course of study completed? What were the examination results? Was the course taken in the candidate's own time or day-release? What has been learned from the course? When dealing with facts the interviewer must get down to specifics.

In addition to listening for answers, the interviewer must be aware of communications the candidate initiates. He/she may volunteer information. Listening also reveals the false note, the bluff or any uneasiness that is sometimes a prelude to evasion.

The ability to sense the meaning of a candidate's statement is a personal skill. This understanding or empathy can be demonstrated to the candidate by a re-phrasing of the content of his/her words. This playback helps greatly in creating and maintaining rapport.

5.2.1.3 The conclusion

This final phase of the interview has the objectives of:

- enabling the candidate to add anything which may have a bearing on their suitability, or to modify or enlarge on any of the answers given
- enabling the candidate to ask any questions relating to the role
- ensuring the candidate is fully aware of the key selling points of the role (competency development/career progression, etc.)
- explaining to the candidate what will happen next (e.g. decision process, time frame, next contact, etc.)
- thanking the candidate for their time and interest.

However well or badly the interview has gone it is important to conclude it in a polite and pleasant manner.

5.2.2 Post-interview follow-up

As soon as is possible after the interview, an assessment should be made. This involves classifying evidence rather than impressions or feelings. When classifying personal qualities, evidence constitutes a statement of what the candidate actually did in a particular situation, not superficial statements relating to hypothetical situations. It is the evidence of current behaviour that is the best predictor of future behaviour.

When classifying specialist qualities, evidence occurs where the candidate has had to go beyond his/her current range of experience and address hypothetical operational situations.

Having classified the evidence, the next stage is evaluation. This must be done against the attributes required and defined in the personal profile.

Once classification and evaluation has taken place, selection can be made (if this opportunity exists). The most 'suitable' candidate should be selected (i.e. the one who matches most closely the requirements of the personal profile).

For each interview a written evaluation report should be produced so that accurate and relevant communication of the result can be given.

Discussion with the candidate(s) should follow. Those not selected should be spoken to first and an explanation and justification given for non-selection. This should be done in a constructive manner and the candidate should be encouraged to seek further opportunities for project experience with guidance being given on those weaknesses that should ideally be improved/worked on.

The selected candidate's strengths and weaknesses are best discussed and considered in preparation for induction into the role, which is the natural follow-on from selection. Further tuning of the role may also be a necessary outcome of the interviewing process.

As can be seen from the above, selection interviews, done properly, take some time to prepare and carry out and therefore should be part of the Project Manager's 'specialist' work, i.e. they are 'doing' work, not just project management work. One point of note is that interviewing is a specialist skill, so take advice or have someone present from the organisation's human resources or personnel department.

5.2.3 Induction

When a newcomer joins a project, it is in project management's interest to ensure that he/she becomes effective as quickly as possible.

The objective of project induction, therefore, is to enable the newcomer to acquire the basic knowledge, experience and skills to become effective in their project role within a pre-determined period.

An induction plan should be prepared (tuned appropriately to reflect the size of project and the number of resources), as this will introduce the newcomer to the way the project will be managed, and will create a professional impression in his/her mind. Naturally, it should be developed before the newcomer joins the project.

The successful candidate's interview records will provide the basis for the building of the induction plan. A properly conducted interview will have identified the candidate's strengths, weaknesses and aspirations, thereby providing a sound platform upon which to build.

The induction plan and process should cover the following:

- The environment – the location of all essential facilities should be provided if required. A small amount of effort expended in providing the basics of a desk, chair, cupboard space, and computer access will pay significant dividends in terms of employee motivation through an early feeling of belonging.
- Job description – the tuned job descriptions should be provided, discussed and understood.
- The people – introductions should be performed, if necessary, but not too many at a time. They should be kept to manageable numbers per day.
- The job and methods to be used should be discussed.
- Development – descriptions of targets, review procedures and execution of the induction plan should be provided.
- The project – an explanation of the background, objectives, scope and current situation should be given.

The first few days should be relatively stress-free and aimed at settling the newcomer into the environment. As the days progress, the intensity should be increased at a rate consistent with the induction objectives, the project requirements and the measured progress against targets.

As a guiding principle, it is important that the newcomer be allowed to display competence early. The induction planner should therefore seek to use identified strengths first, where the project permits. This approach allows the newcomer to contribute to the project early, and to demonstrate their capabilities before moving on to less familiar areas. Wherever possible, tasks should be planned so as to steer a middle path so that they are both challenging and achievable. This allows the newcomer to feel a positive sense of satisfaction through the glow of achievement.

Regular, pre-planned appraisals of progress are vital. During these, the newcomer should be encouraged to voice concerns. Weekly reviews offer a suitable frequency to allow for close monitoring.

Changes to the plan should be allowed for, whether they result from any concerns or because targets have been achieved. Clearly, changes to the induction plan could have implications for the project, and these must be fed back into the Project and Stage Plans.

It is important that the newcomer feels that his/her questions and concerns can be voiced, so somebody should be designated to be available and to listen to these. Perhaps it might be appropriate to establish a mentor, a person of similar rank to the newcomer, made responsible for the success of the newcomer's induction process. The use of a mentor has a number of benefits including:

- relieving the Project Manager of some duties
- giving limited people management experience to non-management staff
- enabling the newcomer to feel that they can talk more freely about problems and concerns
- helping to develop a feeling of belonging in the team
- enabling the Project Manager to be more objective
- increasing the effectiveness of the induction process.

5.3 Summary

Building the project team is not a simple process, even if the team is already in place. As Project Manager, a significant amount of work has to be done to identify the best people for each of the tasks and identify any potential skill gaps.

Project team selection can use the Stage Plans to identify the skills required in the project team(s). This facilitates the selection process to identify the best person for particular work.

When a newcomer joins a project, it is in the Project Manager's interest to ensure that they become effective as quickly as possible. Knowledge of their existing skills and experience and an effective induction programme will enable the newcomer to acquire the basic knowledge, experience and skills to become effective in their project role within a pre-determined period.

6
TEAM PERFORMANCE AND PRODUCT DELIVERY

The previous section identified several important guiding principles that need to be addressed in order to induct people effectively and get them started on the road to efficient and productive work. PRINCE2 has a very effective mechanism for dealing with two of these principles in particular – allowing the newcomer to display competence early and allowing for regular pre-planned appraisals of progress. This mechanism is the Work Package.

In its formal guise, the Work Package is passed from the customer Project Manager to the supplier Team Manager, but the whole formality of this process can be reasonably adapted by using a rational and pragmatic approach.

Work Packages can have varying degrees of sophistication. In addition to the elements described in the Product Description outlines they can also include items like the product dependencies, resource rates, accounting codes, allocated resources and other management information. More importantly, from the induction point of view, defining the deliverables at the appropriate level will assist the newcomer in becoming effective as it is clear what has to be produced. Also, with the definition of reporting frequency and method, the feedback from the newcomer can also be clearly controlled. These two points are discussed in more detail in the next sections.

6.1 Communicating product requirements with Work Packages

As Project Manager you can specify and agree the content of the Work Package with the various customer and supplier Team Managers depending on the type of project environment in which you are working.

At one extreme is the small team, all co-located, with you as the Project Manager. In addition the project team may be familiar and experienced enough with PRINCE2 to understand and use the processes. Here the simplest way to authorise a Work Package is to tell the team to start the product (on the basis that they know where the Product Descriptions and all the source products and plans are). Caution should be exercised with the level of informality. Even in this simple example the authorisation needs to be formalised, if only by means of an e-mail, to ensure the project has an audit trail of the decision being made.

At the other extreme a project using a third-party supplier for product delivery would have to consider the following issues:

- Size of Work Package – If it is too small your supplier will not be able to plan resources very far in advance. If it is too large you may lose track of which products should be started and by when as this would now be in the hands of the supplier's Team Manager.

- Payment structure – Staged payment contracts should be based on the completion of a Work Package. Time and materials-type contracts will be determined by the size of the Work Package issued.

- Level of confidence with supplier – New suppliers need to be treated with care until they have inspired in you a level of reasonable confidence. Trusted suppliers on the other hand may be given free rein.

- Level of risk – The project is under constant threat from risks that usually end up affecting timescale and/or cost. The frequent delivery of products usually reduces risks.

A project may be either a mix of internal and external teams or somewhere in-between. The Project Manager should decide the level of formality required with each Work Package.

6.2 Communicating product progress with Work Packages

Once the Work Package is in place updating progress is usually straightforward. In accepting the Work Package, the supplier team have also accepted the rules under which progress should be recorded. Therefore, to monitor progress, all you have to do is adhere to what you said should be done in the Work Package. There are several ways of dealing with the capture of progress information in PRINCE2. Although the method's primary focus is on the Checkpoint Report, Table 6.1 shows four simple ways that can be successful, depending on the project environment.

Table 6.1 General communication styles in relation to PRINCE2

Method	Advantages	Disadvantages
Project Manager discusses progress with the team at either a team meeting or a chat over the desk. The Project Manager makes notes in the Daily Log and updates the plan directly.	Simple Keeps paperwork to the minimum Brings you face-to-face with the team Provides instant feedback and motivation for the team.	Can be too informal and not focused on project problems Lack of clear audit trail Problems in producing Highlight Reports.

Method	Advantages	Disadvantages
Project Manager discusses progress with the team at either a team meeting or a checkpoint meeting. The Project Manager makes notes, discusses issues and provides direct feedback to the team in terms of any corrective action to be taken. The Project Manager then prepares the Checkpoint Report documenting what actions have been taken.	Simple Keeps paperwork to the minimum Brings you face-to-face with the team Provides instant feedback and motivation for the team.	More work for the Project Manager The Checkpoint Report may miss items where corrective action has been requested, causing problems in the audit trail process. Lack of clear audit trail.
The Team Manager writes the Checkpoint Report based on their knowledge of deliverable progress and they send this to the Project Manager. The Project Manager updates the plan directly and feeds requests back to the Team Manager for clarification or corrective action.	Formal Gains commitment from Team Manager Good audit trail.	Can be too formal and allow project problems to be overlooked Lack of direct feedback to Team Manager. The feedback has to wait until plan is updated Problems in maintaining good control.
The Team Manager updates the Project Manager on a weekly basis via e-mail (or some other communication medium). Every two weeks the Team Manager sits with the Project Manager and they prepare the Checkpoint Report together.	Good for remote teams, especially where distance or cost of travel is a problem Gains commitment from Team Manager Good audit trail.	Lack of direct feedback to Team Manager can be a problem if the Project Manager waits until the bi-weekly checkpoint meeting Problems in maintaining good control, especially on slipping tasks.

Whichever of the above is chosen, you should be careful to focus on the product being created and the method of reporting progress agreed when the Work Package was accepted.

6.3 Monitoring performance

Now that the fundamental infrastructure is in place for capturing the actual progress of both individuals and the team, the Project Manager has to assess if there are any problems to be resolved. Whilst the Stage Plan and, if applicable, the Team Plan will provide the factual data with respect to performance, it will not provide the underlying reasons for the problems.

Even if the underlying data is not currently showing a trend towards poor performance, there are clues that you can look out for before it becomes apparent.

6.3.1 Team performance

An insight into how the team is doing is shown in Table 6.2.

Table 6.2 Team performance

Poorly performing team	Performing team
Argumentative team meetings with hostility and aggressiveness	Expressions of concern made in appropriate ways
Defensiveness when problems arise	Open exchange of information
Power struggles and challenge to roles	No dissension
Cliques and factions forming	Support for each individual member when required
Spread of negative rumours	Constructive criticism
Poor quality end deliverables	Trust
Excessive absenteeism and sickness	
Unnecessary competition and jealousy	

Whilst poor team performance always comes from individuals, the characteristics of a poorly performing team must be addressed as a team problem first, with individual team members' performance being addressed later if necessary.

The root causes of these types of problems can usually be linked back to the environment the team are working in, the status and recognition given to the team, their security and the pressure they are under.

6.3.2 Dealing with difficult team members

After identifying and dealing with team performance issues, you may still have to deal with a problem team member. If you are faced with this issue, then it is vital to identify if it is performance or misconduct you are dealing with before initiating any sort of remedy.

Performance is concerned with assessments against the standards set for a particular role. As part of the selection process a role definition would have been produced for the individual concerned. In addition standards and processes are set out in the Project Initiation Document and quality plan for the project. Performance, therefore, is an assessment of the individual against these criteria and if the criteria are not being met, taking action to see an improvement over a period of time. As an example, it is part of the role definition for the Team Manager to produce an accurate weekly Checkpoint Report. If the Team Manager is consistently late, then plans should be put in place to ensure an improvement in the person's performance.

Misconduct is very different, in that a person has demonstrated a particular unacceptable behaviour. This needs to be corrected, not over a period of time, but immediately.

This two-track system of discipline (one set of discipline options for performance problems and another for misconduct) reflects the fact that misconduct, usually being a wilful act on the part of the employee, is considered a much more serious transgression than a shortfall in performance. Performance problems are often not the direct fault of the employee and can often be corrected with proper training or motivation.

These two tracks reflect the concept of progressive discipline, that is, you should always select the least severe step that results in the behaviour that you want. For example, if your team member responds to a verbal warning and improves as a result that is ideal, you can move on to your next management challenge. However, if they do not respond to a verbal warning, you then progress to the next step – a written warning – and give that a try. The hope is that they will correct their behaviour before you get to more serious steps, such as removing them from the team.

As preparations are made to discipline the employee, a decision has to be made as to whether the behaviours you are trying to correct are performance-related or the result of misconduct. After that has been resolved decide the best way to get your message across. If the transgression is minor – a lack of attention to detail, for example – you may need only to conduct a verbal counselling. However, if an employee is caught sleeping on the job or absenting themself without just cause, you may decide to suspend them without pay for some period of time.

There are two warnings that you must take note of before proceeding further:

- Make sure that the discipline takes place as soon as possible after the transgression occurs. You want to correct your employee's performance before the problem becomes major. You definitely do not want to make discipline an annual event by saving up all your employee's problems for their periodic performance appraisal.
- Your organisation's system for disciplining employees may be somewhat different from the one that we outline here. You are required to work within the system prescribed by the contract between the employee, your firm and the law. Be sure to review your organisation's policies and labour relations practices and procedures before you embark on the task of disciplining your employees.

6.3.3 Steps in dealing with discipline

Table 6.3 outlines the steps to be taken for progressive discipline and the differences between the two tracks of the approach.

Table 6.3 Dealing with discipline

Performance	Misconduct
Verbal counselling: This form of discipline is certainly the most common, and most managers take this step first when they want to correct an employee's performance. Verbal counselling can range from a simple, spontaneous correction performed in the hallway to a more formal, sit-down meeting in your office. Verbal counselling is not normally documented in employees' files.	**Verbal warning:** When your team member's misconduct is minor or a first offence, the verbal warning provides the least severe option for putting your team member on notice that their behaviour will not be tolerated. In many cases of misconduct, a verbal warning that demonstrates to employees that you are aware of the misconduct is all the correction the situation requires.
Written counselling: When employees do not respond favourably to verbal counselling, or when the magnitude of performance problems warrants its use, you should consider written counselling. Written counselling formalises the counselling process by documenting an employee's performance shortcomings in a written memo. Written counselling is presented to an employee in a one-on-one session in the supervisor's office. After the employee has had an opportunity to read the document, verbal discussions regarding the employee's plans to improve their performance ensue. The documentation becomes a part of the employee's personnel files.	**Written warning:** Unfortunately, not all employees get the message when given a verbal warning. So the magnitude of the offence may require that you skip the verbal warning and proceed directly to the written warning. Written warnings signal to employees that you are serious and that you are documenting their behaviour for their personnel files. An employee's immediate supervisor gives the written warning.
Negative performance evaluation: If verbal and written counselling fails to improve your team member's performance, the situation warrants a negative performance evaluation. Of course, because performance evaluations are generally given only annually, if at all, they are not usually very useful for dealing with acute situations. However if you give verbal and written counselling to no avail, negative performance evaluations are the way to go.	**Reprimand:** Repeated or serious misconduct results in a reprimand. A reprimand is generally constructed in the same format as a written warning, but instead of being given by an employee's immediate supervisor, it is given by a manager higher up in the organisation. This is the last chance for an employee to correct their behaviour before suspension, demotion, or termination.

Performance

Demotion: Repeated negative performance evaluations or particularly serious performance shortcomings may warrant demoting your team member to a lower rung on the organisational ladder. Often, but not always, the pay of demoted employees is also reduced at the same time. Unfortunately, some employees are hired or promoted into positions that they just cannot cope with.

This situation is not their fault, but you cannot let a team member continue to fail if you have no hope of bringing performance up to an acceptable level with further training or guidance. Although demoralising, demotions at least allow your employees to move into positions they can handle. Before resorting to demotion, always first try to find a position at an equivalent level that the employee can handle. This will help to improve your employee's motivation and self-confidence and result in a situation that is a win for both the employee and the organisation.

Termination: When all else fails, termination is the ultimate form of discipline for team members who are performing unsatisfactorily. As any manager who has fired anyone knows, terminating someone's employment is difficult and not pleasant.

You should consider it as an option only after you exhaust all other avenues. You must get further advice before embarking on this action from senior management or the organisation's human resources department.

Misconduct

Suspension: A suspension, or mandatory leave without pay, is used in cases of very serious misconduct or repeated misconduct that has not been corrected as a result of other, less severe attempts at employee discipline. You may have to remove employees from the workplace for a period of time to ensure the safety of your other employees or to repair the morale of your team.

Employees may also be given non-disciplinary suspensions while they are being investigated on charges of misconduct. During a non-disciplinary suspension, employees are usually paid while the manager, human resources representative, or other company official reviews the case.

Termination: In particularly serious cases of misconduct, termination may be your first choice in disciplining a worker. This rule is particularly true for extreme violations of safety rules, theft, gross insubordination and other serious misconduct. Termination may also be the result of repeated misconduct that less severe discipline steps do not correct.

6.3.4 Action plan for dealing with discipline

Regardless of which kind of discipline you select for the particular situation, the approach that you should take with your team remains the same. There are five steps that should be taken:

1   Describe the unacceptable behaviour
Exactly what is your team member doing that is unacceptable? When describing

unwanted behaviour, focus on the behaviour and not on the individual and make sure that you are very specific. This is no time for statements such as 'You have a bad attitude', or 'You make a lot of mistakes'.

Always relate unacceptable behaviours to specific performance standards that have not been met or to specific policies that have been broken. Specify exactly what the person did wrong and when the behaviour occurred.

2   Stress the impact to the rest of the team
When people engage in unacceptable behaviour the team is always affected negatively. For example, you may have to assign someone else to cover the team member's position every time they are late. Doing so reduces the efficiency and effectiveness of the team. If it is a case of sexual harassment, the morale and effectiveness of the workers who are subjected to the harassment necessarily suffer.

3   Detail the changes to be made
Tell your team member the exact behaviour that you want them to adopt. This should be in accordance with an established performance standard (possibly their role definition) or company policy.

4   'Or else...'
Of course, no discipline would be complete without a discussion of what is going to happen if the unacceptable behaviour continues. A warning of the consequences of unacceptable performance or misconduct should be given. The message should be clear and unequivocal and the other party should confirm that they understand it.

5   Steps for improvement
Defining the steps a team member has to undertake to improve performance within a fixed period of time is a crucial part of the discipline process.

Steps taken should include:

- clear direction to your staff about what it takes to make satisfactory improvement
- a timetable with a definite completion date and fixed milestones along the way
- any additional resources or training that may be required.

6.4 Managing performance and dealing with non-delivery

Performance can be affected by a number of factors, but if the team is not sufficiently motivated then role definitions and team focusing will be less effective.

The signs of demotivation might be:

- decreased productivity
- more conflict

- increased absenteeism
- poor time-keeping
- an increased error rate (due to lack of attention to detail), etc.

There is no panacea to motivating the team. Different people are motivated by different factors.

- Money – Financial reward may motivate as a 'carrot' but is unlikely to continue to motivate after it has been received.
- Perks – Essentially the same argument applies as for money.
- Authority – Having people report to them may be stimulating for some people.
- Status – Being near the top of the hierarchy is some people's goal.
- Responsibility – Being in charge of people and products and having people relying on them will often result in people making an extra effort.
- Freedom of action – Being in charge of what and/or how things are done can be a powerful incentive.
- Professional pride – Pride in a job well done is a common motivator.
- Clear goals – Unambiguous statements of what is to be done are recognised by many as being very important.
- Public recognition of success might represent an incentive to some people.
- Challenging work – Some people need to have their capabilities stretched to the limit.
- Working environment – A comfortable, convenient and aesthetically pleasing environment plus social factors, such as a good team atmosphere, tend to foster higher levels of motivation.
- Reputation – Some, particularly technical specialists, enjoy the kudos from being an acknowledged expert and being looked up to.
- Personal development – The opportunity to further one's career and/or store of knowledge and experience commonly spurs people on to higher achievement.
- Fear – Either self-generated or supported by threats, may result in short-term increases in output.

An effective manager will identify the appropriate motivating factors for the individuals in the team (since everyone is different) and use them to 'get people to do willingly what they have to do anyway' – a somewhat cynical but perhaps true statement. A detailed discussion on motivation is covered in Section 2.3.

Hints and tips for maintaining momentum

Projects do not exist in a vacuum. They are changing the organisation in some way, which often means that while some people will gain others will lose. Hence there is often resistance to change and that needs to be addressed.

Projects also have to interface with other projects and Project Managers need to raise their heads above the parapet to make this work.

Often business priorities change and the project you are running is then deemed less important than another one. From the project's perspective this is disappointing, particularly if it is suspended and the resources moved elsewhere. The only comfort comes from understanding that, from an organisational perspective, the best use is being made of the scarce funds and your project's turn in the sun may return.

Often major incidents in 'business as usual' will have an effect on projects. For example, a recent incident in a major airline had all projects postponed for a number of days while personnel were drafted to solve an operational problem with ticketing and check-in.

Most of the above scenarios are unavoidable but can cause motivation problems both for the Project Manager and for the team. Watching out for the signs of demotivation and being prepared to respond to them will stop productivity from dropping and affecting the overall success of the project.

In addition to all of the above, it has to be remembered that the natural momentum of a project goes through peaks and troughs. The Project Manager should be aware of this and be prepared to ensure that progress is maintained during 'grind' phases and control and quality are kept up in phases when the team is raring to forge ahead. The beginning of a project is exciting; it is new, the specialist work is just starting and the team has high expectations. At the end people are thinking about their next project and desperate to finish the current one. There is an impending sense of achievement, which keeps motivation high.

During the middle part of the project, people often feel stuck in the doldrums with the 'light at the end of the tunnel' a long way off. Often they are finding more problems than solutions and sometimes feel that the 'light at the end of the tunnel' might actually be a train coming in the opposite direction! Project Managers need to:

- show evidence of progress and communicate to the team that the Project Manager expects the problems, i.e. 'don't worry so much', 'grit your teeth and get on with it';

- consider rewards for continued effort, such as team events, perks or project-sponsored social events. Sometimes team spirit has to be purchased at the bar;

- consider offering bonuses if staff see the project through to the end.

6.5 Conflict and issue management

Conflict is natural and should be encouraged. Disagreements or disputes may reveal opportunities to find a better approach to the project or to build or repair relationships within the project team that may be hampering productivity.

Whether you are involved or the conflict is between others, you can address it in the following manner:

- Be aware of the conflict – As part of the day-to-day management the Project Manager needs to be sensitive to what personal and social tensions there are, without appearing intrusive. Look for body language, tone of voice and talk to your people.

- Decide your business and personal objectives – What are the real business objectives? What are your own personal objectives for the project? Only a clear view of these will enable you to determine whether and how to address the conflict situation.

- Analyse and gather information – The more information you can get together the better prepared you will be to make a decision and take appropriate action.

- Decide whether to take action or not. None is required if it does not affect the business or personal objectives. Make a conscious decision.

- Determine strategy – This may be 'leave well alone', disciplinary action or more usually something in-between. Think carefully about what to do and how to do it and plan it in some detail (location, timing, etc.). If those involved are going on holiday the next day it might be worth waiting until they return. Consider the person's potential reaction and feelings.

- Deal with it assertively – Once you have decided what to do and how, pursue your decision in a strong, positive, assertive way. You may decide to adopt the 'sandwich' approach – 'I was pleased with the way you did…', 'however we need to resolve this problem with…', 'I hope we can sort this out quickly as you are a valuable member of the team and I wouldn't want to lose you'. Think carefully about the approach to the particular situation and the seriousness of it.

- Monitor/reward/readdress – Check that the issue has been, or is being, resolved. Recognise their effort and, if appropriate, express your appreciation.

6.5.1 Resolving conflict

There are some simple steps to follow when thinking about conflict resolution:

- Establish the desired outcome (from the business perspective). Get the people in conflict to agree on what the desired outcome is. If it is handled sensitively, and the aims of the project established as paramount, it could depersonalise the situation, remove some of the negative emotion and focus on the business result.

- Agree on what you agree on. This can be very powerful. If the non-conflict items relevant to the situation can be set out, the 'problem areas' can be seen in context. Frequently the apparent areas of conflict are very few or small and putting them in perspective helps to set a positive tone.

- Compromise. Try to decide what is important and what is less important to each party. You may be able to give concessions on aspects that are less important to you in exchange for similar concessions from the other party and thereby work towards a solution. Items that are important to one party are often less important to the other, hence compromise may lead to an acceptable solution.

- Identify and clarify unresolved points. If agreement cannot be reached get the parties to agree on what cannot be agreed. In itself this can help clarify the ideas and put them into perspective, and allow you to negotiate a resolution or agree the next step. Then, focus on the agreed outcome, try to reach a compromise again and, if not, then agree an escalation route or next action.

- Summarise and agree. Bring the discussion together. This may be formal (e.g. if contractual obligations are involved) or informal. If the conflict could recur or is significant this should be formally documented.

6.6 Losing resources

Despite being the ideal manager and creating a workers' paradise there are many reasons why a project may lose staff. Reasons could include:

- termination of employment with or without notice
- long-term sickness
- internal moves to another project or department.

Before rushing to the resourcing or HR manager to advertise for a replacement, the Project Manager should consider some key questions:

- Was this inevitable, i.e. does the project have a high turnover of staff, or was it prompted by some particular actions? In the case of termination or an internal move, it could be a result of some dispute of which the Project Manager is aware so the loss may be almost expected. Long-term sickness could be related to the pressure placed on the team by the schedule or the nature of the work, in which case there may be an issue for you to address with the Project Board in order to relieve it.

- What is it that the person was working on? Does it require distinct specialist skills or can other people in the team complete their work? The Project Plan and Work Package will help here to identify the scope of the work being undertaken and the progress made. If the work is taken on by other team members, how will this affect their other work and therefore the schedule?

- Will there be an impact on the team as a result of this person leaving? People react differently to these situations and this aspect needs to be considered carefully as it has implications for morale and performance. Without adjusting the schedule, other team members may feel aggrieved at taking on additional work. Relative remuneration levels will also be a factor if the leaver was paid more than the person(s) taking on their work. Departures can also have an impact on anyone new joining the team as the new incumbent may find it hard to match up to the person who has left, especially initially, while getting up to speed with the project and its situation.

- Do we need a replacement and if so what are the skills and personality types the project requires? This may be a golden opportunity to identify a new resource with a specific set of specialist skills to fill gaps in the team. Referring back to Belbin's analysis of team roles it may be an opportunity to co-opt a person of a particular type to fill a role within the team.

Having identified the answers to the above questions, the Project Manager will be in a position to either rearrange assigned work if there is not going to be a replacement person or to follow certain of the steps on building the project team identified in Section 5.2.

6.7 Managing Stage Boundaries

A few years ago there was a spoof notice, in the style of a Samaritans' advert, found pinned to notice boards around the country. It said: 'Are you lonely? Have you no friends? Have you got too much time on your hands? Fret no more, help is here…. Hold a meeting!'

Meetings are expensive. The next time you are in a meeting count the number of attendees and factor in a nominal rate for the duration of the meeting. You will be surprised at the cost.

In the main, meetings are only necessary to

- gain commitment
- build relationships
- negotiate or handle conflict situations
- gather impressions or non-verbal data from body language, etc.

71

They are not required to update Project Plans with progress – progress meetings should be replaced with Checkpoint Reports or, if they are to be held, then a Checkpoint Report should be sent in advance and people only need to discuss the points of debate, questions or dispute.

6.7.1 Communication with the rest of the organisation

During Initiating a Project, you will have produced a Communication Plan. The plan needs to be put into practice, reviewed iteratively to communicate with the host organisation and the messages clearly communicated.

Itemised below are the major considerations in developing a Communications Plan. The extent to which each element will feature depends upon the complexity of the project.

- Identify the stakeholders, both internal and external, their needs, attitudes and characteristics.

- Identify groups of stakeholders as individual audiences, depending on their needs, characteristics or possible reactions, e.g. is a particular group likely to be negative, irrespective of the message, and therefore require particular care?

- Select the senders. It is important to select communicators who have the respect and trust of the audience. Their position in the organisation and expertise in the subject matter will greatly influence their credibility.

- Identify communication vehicles and channels, e.g. face-to-face, e-mail, conferences, road shows, presentations, newsletters, training material. Select channels appropriate to the characteristics and dimensions of the message.

- Identify feedback mechanisms. These should be cost-effective and fit the chosen communications vehicle, e.g. a self-addressed survey card in a newsletter.

- Establish metrics to evaluate the effectiveness of the components of the communications process, e.g. the channels used for communication and feedback.

- Develop a communications process which identifies both roles and responsibilities for communication such as nominating a communications officer and also audience groupings to be communicated with, e.g. user forums.

In general, plan to communicate early and often and maintain communications through all stages of the project, especially at stage boundary time.

6.8 Summary

The subdivision of the project's work into manageable portions is a critical factor for project progress both in terms of its technical management and of the management and motivation of the team. The specification and agreement with the various customer and supplier Team

Managers will determine the content of each Work Package defined by the Project Manager. In the main this will depend on the level of formality and type of project environment. Small co-located teams will require simpler Work Packages than a project using a third-party supplier for product delivery due to potential legal aspects and formality surrounding the work done by external suppliers. The type and size of package will depend in the main on the level of risk involved.

Should progress not measure up to expectations, team performance may somehow be at the root of the problem.

Whilst poor team performance always comes from individuals, the poorly performing team characteristics must be addressed as a team problem first, with the performance of individual team members being dealt with later if required.

After identifying and dealing with team performance issues, you may still have to deal with a problem team member and an action plan for dealing with team members may be required.

Disagreements or disputes within the team may reveal new opportunities to find a better approach to the project or to build or repair relationships within the project team that may be hampering productivity.

7

OTHER PROJECT INITIATION ISSUES

Although no serious analysis has been completed in this area, Project Managers can typically expect to spend up to 80% of the initiation effort discussing requirements, needs, wants, process and procedures. This is reflected in the Initiating a Project processes: planning quality, planning a project and refining the Business Case and risks. The remaining 20% is then split evenly over the rest of the Initiating a Project processes: documenting the results in the initiation document, setting up project controls and setting the project files and other structures. Negotiating and gaining approval are essential elements in this process and, as this section will demonstrate, this is not confined to the authorising a project process.

7.1 Typical people issues

The initiation stage of the project can, from a people point of view, have the following problems:

- Teams providing gold-plated solutions because of misunderstandings about the level of quality required.

- Disagreement about product acceptance due to inadequate and/or ineffective approaches to checking quality.

- Identifying the appropriate control information requirements that will assist monitoring and control of the project whilst minimising the burden on the project team.

7.2 Quality planning

Incorrect assumptions about what constitutes quality on a project have historically been one of the major problems to have impacted on projects.

These assumptions can be made either:

- Arbitrarily, usually without reference to the user. This would typically be because either the suppliers did not perceive that the users needed to become involved, or because the users themselves did not have the time and/or the inclination to do so. Most usually it is because of a mixture of both these reasons.

- Conflicts between the interests of quality, time and cost. People invariably have differing views regarding which should take precedence.

- It can be difficult to identify what quality aspects are important because people will not commit to a definite decision.

The situation is alleviated somewhat within the PRINCE2 environment, because the product's eventual users are required to be involved in the management of the project from an early stage. Even so, this involvement does not mean that the necessary definition of the product's desired attributes (or qualities) is explored and agreed at the outset. It is a project management function that makes this happen.

The start point in project quality planning must be to derive a list of relevant quality requirements for a project, and to use this as a basis to establish relative priorities for those requirements. Without this prioritisation it may be difficult or impossible to resolve potential conflicts.

If, for example, a building was required to be both easy to enter but also secure, during the design stage these two requirements might be found to be in conflict.

It would clearly be wrong in this case for the product builder to assume that, for example, security was more important than ease of access – that is the customer's decision. Sadly, and all too often, the wrong people make assumptions like this. The existence of a prioritised list of desired product qualities provides the product builders with unambiguous information to resolve conflicts of this kind.

It is important that this list of desired qualities is not just derived from the product's user. A representative of the business itself has to be consulted in order to ensure that the cost of providing certain quality attributes in a product is justified by their consequent benefits to the organisation. The business voice, through both the Project Board and corporate/programme management will also provide direction in other areas, such as helping to ensure that the qualities desired by the user are in line with the organisation's overall direction, strategy, policies, image, etc.

Figure 7.1 shows that there are other views to be taken into account when deriving the quality requirements of the project. These include the specialists, i.e. the product builders, or their representatives, possibly through the supplier's quality management system, who must be consulted during quality specification. As specialists, they are best placed to advise whether the desired qualities are achievable or not.

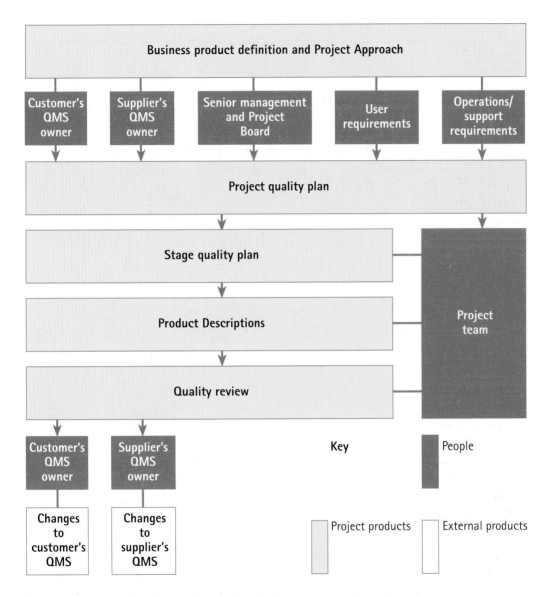

Figure 7.1 Impact of quality on the relationship between products and people

The diagram also shows the relationship between the quality management system (QMS) and the business product for both the customer and, if appropriate, the supplier.

The Project Manager must create a working relationship with the owner of the QMS. This will ensure there is a well-defined link between business products being produced and the QMS.

7.3 Avoiding conflict in discussions about quality

Despite using the word 'quality' frequently in our lives, trying to define what we mean by quality can be difficult. To avoid problems with those in the quality defining process, it is probably not a good idea to start with the general question 'What quality do we want for this product?'

Below is a list of topics that may be used to stimulate thoughts about the type of questions that should be asked with a view to achieving a hierarchy of importance:

Efficiency	What does the customer consider efficiency to be, and does the product conform to this?
Reliability	What will the measurement for reliability be and to what extent will the product need to conform to this in terms of features like stability, dependability, reputability, etc.?
Maintainability	Is it easy to change, service and repair?
Speed	Does it function at the required speed?
Timeliness	Can it be provided at any time, giving optimum benefits at optimum cost?
Safety	Is it safe to install, operate and maintain and to what safety legislation will it need to conform?
Legislation	Does it need to conform to other legal requirements? If so, which ones?
Capacity	Can the product accommodate the required throughput and will it be able to deal with predicted operational peaks and troughs?
Growth	Will the product be able to deal with anticipated changes in the throughput requirements?
Standards	Does the product conform to the customer's standards?
Image	Does the product reflect the image that the customer wishes to project?
Cost	Is it within the customer's expectations and requirements for purchase price and operational running costs?
Benefits	Will the product bring to the customer the optimum benefits at an optimum cost?

Some of the above may be relevant and important to the customer, others may be less so. The product supplier will almost certainly be unable to predict accurately the requirements and priorities. It is necessary to form a partnership between customer and supplier in order to define truly what product quality really means in detail. Basing the discussion around objective indicators of quality and performance can circumvent issues of perception or perspective and take potential heat out of discussions on quality.

7.4 Checking quality

Just as the Work Package was accepted from the Project Manager, notification of its completion must be returned to the Project Manager.

The configuration management system used by the project may handle the return of the actual products of the Work Package. The Team Manager must ensure that the products are handed over correctly and advise the Project Manager that the hand-over has occurred.

The process has three elements:

- Obtain sign-off by any required quality checkers for the products developed.
- Hand over the completed products.
- Advise the Project Manager that the Work Package is now complete.

As before, the methods of achieving these elements should have been defined as part of the Work Package authorisation.

Checking the quality of a product has many people issues bound up in it: acceptance or otherwise is a reflection on the contribution(s) of team members. Individually and as a team there is pride, skill, reputation and motivation at stake if the quality is found to be short of the desired level. Similarly though, failing to meet a deadline may be viewed as a visible failure and create the temptation to hand in 'any old thing' just to meet the deadlines.

All products have to be checked against their quality criteria. The types of quality control techniques employed within a project will vary enormously, depending on the nature of the project and its products. Below are some of the more commonly used quality control techniques used in projects:

- testing
- inspection
- walk-through.

Quality review is the main PRINCE2 technique that is explained in detail in the manual. Whatever technique is employed, the manner of communicating the assessment will have a bearing on the people-related issues mentioned above so it has to be handled with due forethought.

A quality review, as the PRINCE2 manual describes, is a meeting whose purpose is to identify deficiencies in a product against its Product Description. PRINCE2 calls discrepancies errors, but the term 'discrepancy' is more in keeping with the recommended approach founded on constructive tact and diplomacy.

Bearing these facts in mind, from the Project Manager's point of view, there are some golden rules for making quality review work.

- Many organisations have had trouble making quality review work, because they fail to adopt the right psychological or cultural approach.

- Tact and diplomacy (like good manners) cost nothing and can contribute enormously to a positive outcome.

- The outcome of any review is that ownership of the result is shared. In other words, the producer was the psychological owner before the meeting, whereas after the meeting all the participants are owners, each having contributed their share. A problem discovered with the product subsequently is the joint responsibility of the entire group, not just the producer. The words 'us', 'we' and 'our' instead of 'you' and 'yours' help to promote this attitude.

- The reviewers should take care to assess the product, not the producer – All remarks should be presented in terms of improving the product, not attacking its author.

- Often, when the project or organisational culture is not right, the quality review turns into a parody of a courtroom with the chair, reviewers and producer taking the roles of judge, jury and accused. This will inevitably cause problems.

- The main aim of the quality review meeting is to agree and record discrepancies. It is easy to get distracted from this, but all participants should be conscious of the need to stick to the point.

- Thorough preparation is vital (remember that the question lists need to get back to the producer in good time). Time must be allocated and used for thorough preparation.

- Discrepancy identification not solutions – If the preparation has been done properly, then the quality review meeting should just be a matter of agreeing and recording discrepancies. If the participants start trying to fix the discrepancies, i.e. say what needs to be done, then the time will soon ebb away. It may be useful to allow a very short period of discussion on solutions, if deemed appropriate by the chair, but this should be kept to a minimum.

- Avoid the trivial – Remember to avoid picking on unimportant issues in the meeting.

- Non-participants excluded – Some meetings have numerous 'interested parties' attend, notably the line managers of the participants. This contributes nothing to the effectiveness of the meeting and is best avoided.

- Fifty pages maximum – In a two-hour meeting, it is unlikely that more than this number of pages can be properly reviewed. If your document resembles *War and Peace* remember how difficult it would be to review hundreds of pages at a sitting. Proper stage planning can help avoid this scenario by identifying a more realistic 'chunk' of work. Where a large document has to be reviewed, then several sittings may be necessary.

- Get expert reviewers – Where the reviewers are not (technically) up to the job, the most likely outcome is that they will concentrate on trivia and miss the important points.

7.5 Setting up project controls

An effective project control system relies on two fundamental components:

- a plan against which progress can be measured (and new circumstances evaluated), and
- timely and accurate information about what is actually happening (or likely to happen) on the project.

It therefore goes without saying that any project control system can only ever be as good as the current information that is available to it, regardless of how good the original plan might have been.

7.5.1 Capturing data

Capturing data about time spent by individuals working on a project (as is often done via time sheets or work records which refer to activities) should be a straightforward task requiring very little thought. Capturing accurate and meaningful information about what is really happening, and what is about to happen on the project may be a different matter entirely, because people working on a demanding project, or one with tight timescales, quickly forget exactly what they were doing a week ago. Perhaps more critically, products with short development times (two or three days) can slip by 100% or more before the slippage is formally reported.

One final and important issue relating to the recording of time and effort is that of the need for accuracy, as in 'truth'. For a variety of reasons, product developers may record effort and times that do not reflect reality. They may under-quote 'estimates to complete' for reasons of optimism or a wish to avoid causing unnecessary problems. Equally, there is sometimes a temptation to over-quote the effort expended to date on a product because organisational standards stipulate that a certain percentage of their time must be booked to productive work.

There may also be a tendency to ignore work done in overtime (paid or otherwise) and this can introduce large errors into what are supposed to be accurate statements of effort expended.

Whatever the circumstances it is the responsibility of the Project Manager, or in some cases Team Manager, to ensure that the information provided is as accurate as possible, and that the project's control mechanisms actively encourage this.

7.5.2 Ongoing communication

In addition to gathering the information needed to evaluate progress against the Stage Plan the data capture process (or procedures) should also aim to obtain other types of information that might be loosely described as 'intelligence'. It should cover any information that can be used to explain why things have happened and identify trends or anything else that may assist in managing the project. Information in this category should include:

- the reason for early or late product completion
- the reason for changes to original estimates of effort, time or costs (known as variances)
- revised views of known risks and anticipated problems
- identification and explanation of unplanned activities
- changes to the expected availability of project resources.

This is by no means an exhaustive list but suffices to indicate the type of information required. Commonly, much of this information is discovered during conversations between the Project Manager and team members, and from other sources in an equally informal manner, such as from checkpoint meetings.

7.5.3 Approaches to data collection

This informal approach has the merit of imposing minimal overheads on the project in terms of procedures and paperwork. On the other hand it suffers from the risk that people will quickly forget things that are not related to their immediate task, will make their own judgements about what issues matter most and may not even consider some aspects of the project unless they are prompted. On a small project with a team of only three or four people these risks may be considered sufficiently small to justify doing without any formal procedures. Where a project involves 20 people or more the risks are much greater and a more formal approach should be considered.

This emphasis on formality should not, however, be automatically taken to mean more paperwork. Standard forms may be desirable for some projects and some organisations, and this may be especially true of projects in the following circumstances:

- the team members are working in two or more physically separate locations

- a proportion of the project's products are being developed by external contractors, who may also be at a remote location

- some (or all) members of the project team are inexperienced and cannot be expected to know what information may be significant

- some members of the team, whilst experienced in their own area of the organisation, may not be aware of the implications of events for aspects of the project relating to other areas. This is often true for business users working on an IT development project, and possibly even more true for any IT staff who are not intimately familiar with the users' environment.

However, even if all these circumstances applied, an equally effective procedure might simply involve polling Team Managers and team members at regular intervals with a checklist of questions. As in so many other aspects of project control the rigour and formality of the procedures adopted should reflect a realistic assessment of the risks associated with the project and the complexity of the management task.

7.6 Summary

Having incorrect assumptions about quality at the start of a project does not only impact the product being produced.

Anger and frustration as a result of having to change one's view about the level of quality for each of the project's products can be the result of poor quality planning.

Even with a good plan in place, not checking products against the definition of acceptability of the major problems can also impact the motivation of the team.

It is a project management function that makes this happen.

The start point in project quality planning must be to derive a list of relevant quality requirements for the result from a project, and to use this as a basis to establish relative priorities for those requirements.

The PRINCE2 use of Work Packages helps to avoid these problems by defining the parameters and types of quality control techniques employed for each product before work commences. This enables the resources building products to be clear about what is required of them, saving both time and frustration in the checking and hand-over process.

This section has also looked at another issue to be addressed during project initiation, that is setting up project controls.

It is the responsibility of the Project Manager, or in some cases Team Manager, to ensure that

- the information provided from the chosen controlling mechanism is as accurate as possible
- these actively encourage the team to produce accurate information
- there is as little overhead as possible on the resources being asked to supply the information.

Standard forms may be desirable for some projects and some organisations but an effective approach could be as simple as 'tell me in less than half a page where we are'.

8

PROJECT CLOSURE AND PLANNING GOODBYE

This section deals with how the PRINCE2 Closing a Project process impacts on people and the issues that can materialise from the three triggers that cause a project to enter this process:

- Closure by the Project Board
- Closure by exception
- Closure by completion.

8.1 Closure by the Project Board

One of the benefits of having the Project Board in place is that it has access to the wider business. This gives it access to information not normally available to Project Managers. There will therefore be occasions when the Project Manager is called by the Executive and told that despite the project still being within Tolerance, the Business Case has changed and therefore the project is no longer required.

The Project Manager now has to plan the closure of the project, including the deliverables, as specified in the PRINCE2 manual, e.g. archive of products, Lessons Learned Reports, etc. There are also people issues to resolve, usually on two levels: what to do from a resource owner's view and what to say to the individual team members.

8.1.1 Resource owner issues

In project close down situations all of the resources (which, for the purposes of this book, means the people) have to be sent back from where they came as soon as possible. The plan for project closure and knowledge of the contractual situation for each person will help. However, the situation will at some stage have to be discussed with each of the resource owners.

Resource owners are usually one of the following:

- Internal resource manager. These are resource owners/staff members from within the organisation. As there is usually plenty of work to do within an organisation, internal resource owners are usually easy to deal with as they can utilise the freed additional resources quickly.
- An agent (usually for a contract worker or a team of contractors). Agents supply a

specialist resource for a fixed period of time (typically three months minimum). The business structure for agents is based on a percentage fee of the daily rate for each person supplied.

- A consultancy. The project may have hired a set of specialist skills from an organisation, e.g. a testing team. The fee structure may be based on either a daily rate for each person, cost plus, i.e. the cost of the person to the owner company plus a management fee or a fixed price.

- Third-party supplier. Third-party suppliers, in general, have bid for the work and will supply sufficient resources to complete the commitment. In these situations a supplier may be left with resources unused as well as unused materials bought in to produce the products.

Having identified who the resource owners are the next problem to negotiate is the release of the resources. This should be carefully planned and using the following steps may ease the process.

- Decide what the business problem is and focus on the project, not the people. This will usually come down to a monetary value. However, it is more difficult to do this if the discussion is related to personalities.

- Consider the other side's position and try to see the situation from their point of view. If you need to continue a working relationship with them you may well need to find a solution that allows them to save face but may not be ideal for you.

- Work out how to deal with the situation assertively in terms of approach, body language, place, timing, and saying clearly what you want. However, it is important when you are personally involved not to be aggressive (or passive).

- Be aware of, and manage, your own likely reactions. Think about your emotions, stay in control, and keep the approach assertive. You need to know yourself.

- Plan the encounter. Having worked out what to do and how to deal with it, maximise your chances of success by detailed planning and ensuring you keep control of the exchange. Decide the style you will adopt in the encounter.

All of the above points must be considered in conjunction with the Senior Supplier(s) on the Project Board. If they are one of the resource owners then this will be an easier task, as they will already be aware of the premature close. In some situations it may be more acceptable if the Senior Supplier, or possibly the Executive, completes the negotiations. This may be appropriate where an existing long-term relationship with a supplier may be damaged by an early project closure or where the 'position power' of senior management may help with credibility or influence in the negotiations. Here the Project Manager will take a back seat in the discussion or no further part, depending on the Board's decision.

8.2 Closure by exception

In closure by exception, something has happened on the project, making closure appropriate. Either Tolerances have been exceeded or there is an issue that cannot be resolved. These manifest themselves as one of the following:

- Change in benefits
- Products cannot be delivered as specified
- Products will exceed planned cost or time
- Issues, requests for change or off-specifications have been raised.

For some team members this will not be a surprise, especially those closely connected with the product or issue. For others, however, it may come as a shock.

In these situations the Project Manager will have discussed the exception with either the Project Board or the Executive and prepared an Exception Report. Based on this report the Project Board can recommend closure, especially after discarding all viable options.

As far as the required activities, issues and sensitivities are concerned, closure by exception is functionally the same situation as described earlier, that is closure by the Project Board.

8.3 Closure by completion

Closure by completion is the close of the project by delivery and acceptance of all specified project products.

Planning for the next stage involves identifying products, risks, resources and costs for each of the products on the Stage Plan. Planning for project completion is no different except that the final project stage has to deliver the products specified in the PRINCE2 project closure process. These include:

- End project notification
- End Project Report
- Lessons Learned Report
- Follow-on Action Recommendations
- Post-Project Review Plan.

In addition the Project Manager has to include details of how to close down the project successfully, which from a people perspective includes release of all resources used on the project (including yourself as Project Manager). Before we go on to discuss these points there are two key products with people aspects that will need updating. The first of these is the Communication Plan, the second is the Risk Log.

8.3.1 Updating the Communication Plan for closure

The Communication Plan was produced way back in the initiation stage. When planning the final stage of the project it is important to take a fresh look at the Communication Plan and check that it covers:

- all resourcing managers and how they will be notified of the release of their resources, and

- how closure will be communicated to the project team, third-party suppliers, users and the rest of the organisation.

It is likely that the early plan did not cater for these two points, either because they were a totally unknown factor or lacked importance at the stage in the project when the plan was produced. Updating the plan or re-reading it ahead of closure affords the opportunity to consider, refine and rehearse the activities implied by closure ahead of the real event and in the light of the circumstances.

8.3.2 Updating the Risk Log

The Risk Log is reviewed during Managing Stage Boundaries, capturing risks present in the next Stage Plan and closing risks associated with products just delivered.

There are risks specifically associated with the people side of project closure that should be added to the Risk Log.

Early leavers present one such risk. During the last stage of a project more than at any other time staff will typically leave before they are scheduled to.

- When an organisation recognises that a project is nearly finished it can sometimes lead to a belief that the project cannot possibly need as much anymore, or cannot need a particular resource. This can be especially true when there is a new, exciting project just beginning.

- In addition, contract staff need to keep working as no work means no income. During the last stage of the project, contract resources will be looking for their next piece of work and if their search is successful this may present them with a choice. Should they accept a new contract that will keep them employed for the next six months or turn it down and stay with their current project for the last few weeks? According to Maslow's hierarchy of needs, survival is a more basic requirement than belonging, so in this example having an income would probably override any desire to remain a part of their present team.

Both of these points introduce a schedule risk to the project, inasmuch as there may be insufficient resources to deliver the products as planned. Moreover, from a people point of view the risk is that early leavers can:

- upset the balance of the team
- demotivate remaining team members
- cause loss of specialist product or business knowledge.

Each of these can create problems for the productivity of the team.

Another risk to be considered is the final review and delivery of specified products to the customer. Products, despite best efforts, always have problems in final overall testing or integration into existing environments. This goes beyond passing or failing the quality review, stretching into uncharted areas that may not even have been thought of.

From a people perspective there are various issues:

- The team is under pressure to fix any new, unexpected problems.
- The team is also under pressure to deliver the remaining project products to the existing schedules.
- The team, or some members of the team, may start to work excessive hours in order to cope with fixing and continuing delivery.

Failure to identify these risks during the planning of the final stage can start a self-reinforcing downward spiral in the team.

Strategies for dealing with this problem are in themselves problematic. For example, one approach may be to bring in the support team for the live product early and use them to fix problems. This may have an additional advantage of support becoming familiar with the product early. However, it does carry the risk of loss of confidence in the end product if there are major problems found. Whichever approach is chosen it should be remembered that in the main people have pride in their work and hate to deliver 'problem' products. This can be the key difficulty that has to be addressed.

8.3.3 Last stage/closure people issues

The previous paragraphs identified some of the people problems associated with the last stage of the project leading to closure, including the effect on the team of early leavers and the pressure of continued delivery whilst dealing with problems with completed products.

There are additional challenges for the Project Manager in this period associated with maintaining motivation and therefore the productivity of the project team.

- 'Loose ends' work is notoriously difficult and frustrating to complete. Loose ends include all those 'drudgery jobs' that people put off because they were thought not to be important at the time. Favourite loose ends include technical documentation, user guides, and support documentation, etc.

- Loose ends work is tedious when compared with the excitement of delivering what is considered to be the real product. The Project Manager's role here is to lead the resource (leading in the sense of making people do willingly what they have to do anyway) by stressing the importance of the work and (if it is true) the skills they possess that are essential for its successful completion.

- 'No work' or slack periods are common towards the end of a project. This is when the project team (not necessarily the whole team) is needed but there is not always work for all of them. This may occur during the last stages of acceptance testing, where the users are very busy, and the developers and testers are not fully occupied but are still required to resolve issues users identify. The simple solution is to get the team to do the loose ends work during this time. This will go some way to resolving the problem.

There is one other thing that the Project Manager can do for the team; that is, help them to leave the project! The next section describes how this can be done.

8.4 Closing down project resources

This section applies to all three types of project closure described in earlier paragraphs. These essential tasks ideally need to be planned but that is probably only possible in the event of closure by completion. In the other closure scenarios it is paramount that you set aside time for the activities described here.

One of the most important documents that everyone should keep up-to-date at all times is a curriculum vitae. Project Managers should be discussing with the team the status of their CVs and allowing time for updating during the slack periods identified above. By tasking the team in this way, you can be checking the CV update is based on the knowledge, experience and skills learnt and demonstrated on the project. Whilst this may at first seem an odd thing to do, the chances are that some members of the team will be working for you again in the future on another project.

As Project Manager you are not excluded from this updating task for your own curriculum vitae. You will very soon be moving on from the project as well.

Another aspect of work that needs to be thought of in this area is the development of a 'moving on plan'. This may include discussions with the team member to review aspirations, ensuring discussions are held between them and their line or resourcing manager, updating appraisals where appropriate and preparing termination letters for each team member.

8.4.1 Planning your own departure

As stated above, updating your own curriculum vitae is an important end-of-project activity.

In addition to this you should be discussing your own performance with the Project Board and getting them to write a termination and, if appropriate, reference letter for your work in delivering the project.

At this stage you should not be afraid of asking for more work, particularly from the Executive, who may be ready to start another project.

8.5 Summary

This section deals with how the PRINCE2 Closing a Project process identifies the issues and impacts on people that materialise from Closing a Project.

Whichever route is chosen for closing the project, the Project Manager has now to plan carefully, addressing the needs of other stakeholders (resource managers for example).

In addition to the set of PRINCE2 closure products, the Project Manager has to include details of how to release all resources used on the project.

There are specific risks that need to be considered and, if appropriate, controlling actions taken to avoid demotivating the remaining team members.

Project Managers should be discussing with the team the status of their CVs and allowing time for updating during the slack periods in the Project Plan. In addition to this, your own departure and onward move is as valid a project closure deliverable as any other and deserves equal planning effort.

BIBLIOGRAPHY

Adair, J (1983)
Effective Leadership
Gower, Aldershot

Adair, J (1986)
Effective Teambuilding
Gower, Aldershot

Adair, J (1997)
Leadership Skills
Institute of Personnel and Development, London

Belbin, M (1993)
Team Roles at Work
Butterworth Heinnemann, Oxford

Belbin, J (1994)
Management Teams: Why they succeed or fail
Butterworth Heinnemann, Oxford

Blanchard, K (1995, 2000)
One Minute Manager series
HarperCollins

Brooks, F P (1995)
The Mythical Man-month
Addison Wesley Longman

Handy, C (1993)
Understanding Organisations
Penguin, London

Herzberg, F, Mausner, B, and Snyderman BB (1959)
The Motivation to Work
Wiley, New York

Hodgson, J and Hodgson P (1993)
Effective Meetings
Random House

Kolb, DA and Fry, R (1975)
'Towards an Applied Theory of Experiential Learning' in
Cooper, CL (ed)
Theories of Group Processes
John Wiley, London

McCartney, I (2001)
Successful IT: Modernising government in action

McCormack, M (1996)
McCormack on Communicating
Random House

McGregor, D (1960)
Human Side of Enterprise, The
McGraw Hill, New York

Maslow, A (1954)
Motivation and Personality
Harper and Row, New York

Mintzberg, H (1975)
'The Manager's Job: Folklore and fact' in
Harvard Business Review

Morris, P and Hough, G (1987)
The Anatomy of Major Projects
John Wiley, Oxford

OGC (2002)
Managing Successful Projects with PRINCE2
TSO (The Stationery Office)

Toffler, A (1971)
Future Shock
Pan Books, London

Tuckman, B and Jensen, M (1977)
Stages of Small Group Development Revisited
Groups and Organisations Studies

Video Arts (1991)
So You Think You Can Manage?
Mandarin

GLOSSARY

Acceptance Criteria
A prioritised list of criteria that the final product(s) must meet before the customer will accept them; a measurable definition of what must be done for the final product to be acceptable to the customer. They should be defined as part of the Project Brief and agreed between customer and supplier no later than the project initiation stage. They should be documented in the Project Initiation Document.

Activity network
A flow diagram showing the activities of a plan and their interdependencies. The network shows each activity's duration, earliest start and finish times and float. Also known as 'planning network'. *See also* Critical path.

Baseline
A snapshot, a position or situation that is recorded. Although the position may be updated later, the baseline remains unchanged and available as a reminder of the original state and as a comparison against the current position. Products that have passed their quality checks and are approved are baselined products. Anything 'baselined' should be under version control in configuration management and 'frozen', i.e. no changes to that version are allowed.

Benefits
The positive outcomes, quantified or unquantified, that a project is being undertaken to deliver, and that justify the investment.

Benefits realisation
The practice of ensuring that the outcome of a project produces the projected benefits claimed in the Business Case.

Business Case
Information that describes the justification for setting up and continuing a PRINCE2 project. It provides the reasons (and answers the question 'Why?') for the project. It is updated at key points throughout the project.

Change authority
A group to which the Project Board may delegate responsibility for the consideration of requests for change. The change authority is given a budget and can approve changes within that budget.

Change budget

The money allocated to the change authority to be spent on authorised requests for change.

Change control

The procedure to ensure that the processing of all Project Issues is controlled, including the submission, analysis and decision-making.

Checkpoint

A team-level, time-driven review of progress, usually involving a meeting.

Checkpoint Report

A progress report of the information gathered at a checkpoint meeting, which is given by a team to the Project Manager and provides reporting data as defined in the Work Package.

Communication Plan

Part of the Project Initiation Document describing how the project's stakeholders and interested parties will be kept informed during the project.

Concession

An Off-Specification that is accepted by the Project Board without corrective action.

Configuration audit

A comparison of the latest version number and status of all products shown in the configuration library records against the information held by the product authors.

Configuration management

A discipline, normally supported by software tools, that gives management precise control over its assets (for example, the products of a project), covering planning, identification, control, status accounting and verification of the products.

Configuration status account

A report on the status of products. The required products can be specified by identifier or the part of the project in which they were developed.

Contingency budget

The amount of money required to implement a contingency plan. If the Project Board approves a contingency plan, it would normally set aside a contingency budget, which would only be called upon if the contingency plan had to be implemented.

Contingency plan

A plan that provides an outline of decisions and measures to be taken if defined circumstances, outside the control of a PRINCE2 project, should occur.

Critical path

This is the line connecting the start of a planning network with the final activity in that network through those activities with the smallest float. Often this is a line through the network connecting those activities with a zero float, i.e. those activities where any delay will delay the time of the entire network.

Customer
The person or group who commissioned the work and will benefit from the end results.

Deliverable
An item that the project has to create as part of the requirements. It may be part of the final outcome or an intermediate element on which one or more subsequent deliverables are dependent. According to the type of project, another name for a deliverable is 'product'.

End Project Report
A report given by the Project Manager to the Project Board, that confirms the hand-over of all products and provides an updated Business Case and an assessment of how well the project has done against its Project Initiation Document.

End stage assessment
The review by the Project Board and Project Manager of the End Stage Report to decide whether to approve the next Stage Plan (unless the last stage has now been completed). According to the size and criticality of the project, the review may be formal or informal. The approval to proceed should be documented as an important management product.

End Stage Report
A report given by the Project Manager to the Project Board at the end of each management stage of the project. This provides information about the project performance during the stage and the project status at stage end.

Exception
A situation where it can be forecast that there will be a deviation beyond the Tolerance levels agreed between Project Manager and Project Board (or between Project Board and corporate or programme management, or between a Team Manager and the Project Manager).

Exception assessment
This is a meeting of the Project Board to approve (or reject) an Exception plan.

Exception plan
This is a plan that often follows an Exception Report. For a Stage Plan exception, it covers the period from the present to the end of the current stage. If the exception were at a project level, the Project Plan would be replaced.

Exception Report
A report that describes an exception, provides an analysis and options for the way forward and identifies a recommended option. The Project Manager presents it to the Project Board.

Executive

The single individual with overall responsibility for ensuring that a project or programme meets its objectives and delivers the projected benefits. This individual should ensure that the project or programme maintains its business focus, that it has clear authority and that the work, including risks, is actively managed. The chairperson of the Project Board, representing the customer and owner of the Business Case.

Feasibility study

A feasibility study is an early study of a problem to assess if a solution is feasible. The study will normally scope the problem, identify and explore a number of solutions and make a recommendation on what action to take. Part of the work in developing options is to calculate an outline Business Case for each as one aspect of comparison.

Follow-on Action Recommendations

A report that can be used as input to the process of creating a Business Case/Project Mandate for any follow-on PRINCE2 project and for recording any follow-on instructions covering incomplete products or outstanding issues. It also sets out proposals for a Post-Project Review of the project's products.

Gantt chart

This is a diagram of a plan's activities against a time background, showing start and end times and resources required.

Gate review

A generic term, rather than a PRINCE2 term, meaning a point at the end of a stage or phase where a decision is made whether to continue with the project. In PRINCE2 this would equate to an end stage assessment.

Highlight Report

Report from the Project Manager to the Project Board on a time-driven frequency on stage progress.

Issue Log

A log of all Project Issues including requests for change raised during the project, showing details of each issue, its evaluation, what decisions about it have been made and its current status.

Lessons Learned Report

A report that describes the lessons learned in undertaking the project and that includes statistics from the quality control of the project's management products. It is approved by the Project Board and then held centrally for the benefit of future projects.

Off-Specification

Something that should be provided by the project, but currently is not (or is forecast not to be) provided. This might be a missing product or a product not meeting its specification.

Outcome
The term used to describe the totality of what the project is set up to deliver, consisting of all the specialist products. For example, this could be an installed computer system with trained staff to use it, backed up by new working practices and documentation, a refurbished and equipped building with all the staff moved in and working, or it could be a new product launched with a recruited and trained sales and support team in place.

Peer review
Peer reviews are specific reviews of a project or any of its products where personnel from within the organisation and/or from other organisations carry out an independent assessment of the project. Peer reviews can be done at any point within a project but are often used at stage-end points.

Phase
A part, section or segment of a project, similar in meaning to a PRINCE2 stage. The key meaning of stage in PRINCE2 terms is the use of management stages, i.e. sections of the project to which the Project Board only commits one at a time. A phase might be more connected to a time slice, change of skills required or change of emphasis.

Post-implementation review
See Post-project review.

Post-Project Review
One or more reviews held after project closure to determine if the expected benefits have been obtained. Also known as 'post-implementation review'.

PRINCE2
A method that supports some selected aspects of project management. The acronym stands for **PR**ojects **IN** **C**ontrolled **E**nvironments.

PRINCE2 project
A project whose product(s) can be defined at its start sufficiently precisely so as to be measurable against predefined metrics and that is managed according to the PRINCE2 method.

Process
That which must be done to bring about a particular outcome, in terms of information to be gathered, decisions to be made and results that must be achieved.

Producer
This role represents the creator(s) of a product that is the subject of a quality review. Typically, it will be filled by the person who has produced the product or who has led the team responsible.

Product

Any input to or output from a project. PRINCE2 distinguishes between management products (which are produced as part of the management or quality processes of the project) and specialist products (which are those products that make up the final deliverable). A product may itself be a collection of other products.

Product-based planning

A three-step diagrammatic technique leading to a comprehensive plan based on creation and delivery of required outputs. The technique considers prerequisite products, quality requirements and the dependencies between products.

Product Breakdown Structure

A hierarchy of all the products to be produced during a plan.

Product Checklist

A list of the major products of a plan, plus key dates in their delivery.

Product Description

A description of a product's purpose, composition, derivation and quality criteria. It is produced at planning time, as soon as the need for the product is identified.

Product Flow Diagram

A diagram showing the sequence of production and interdependencies of the products listed in a Product Breakdown Structure.

Programme

A portfolio of projects selected, planned and managed in a co-ordinated way.

Project

A temporary organisation that is created for the purpose of delivering one or more business products according to a specified Business Case.

Project Assurance

The Project Board's responsibilities to assure itself that the project is being conducted correctly.

Project Brief

A description of what the project is to do; a refined and extended version of the Project Mandate, which has been agreed by the Project Board and which is input to project initiation.

Project closure notification

Advice from the Project Board to inform the host location that the project resources can be disbanded and support services, such as space, equipment and access, demobilised.

Project closure recommendation

Notification prepared by the Project Manager for the Project Board to send (when the Board is satisfied that the project can be closed) to any organisation that has supplied facilities to the project.

Project Initiation Document (PID)
A logical document which brings together the key information needed to start the project on a sound basis and to convey that information to all concerned with the project.

Project Issue
A term used to cover either a general issue, query, a Request for Change, suggestion or Off-Specification raised during a project. Project Issues can be about anything to do with the project.

Project management
The planning, monitoring and control of all aspects of the project and the motivation of all those involved in it to achieve the project objectives on time and to the specified cost, quality and performance.

Project Management team
A term to represent the entire management structure of Project Board, Project Manager, plus any Team Manager, Project Assurance and Project Support roles.

Project Manager
The person given the authority and responsibility to manage the project on a day-to-day basis to deliver the required products within the constraints agreed with the Project Board.

Project Mandate
Information created externally to the project, which forms the terms of reference and is used to start up the PRINCE2 project.

Project Plan
A high-level plan showing the major products of the project, when they will be delivered and at what cost. An initial Project Plan is presented as part of the Project Initiation Document. This is revised as information on actual progress appears. It is a major control document for the Project Board to measure actual progress against expectations.

Project Quality Plan
A plan defining the key quality criteria, quality control and audit processes to be applied to project management and specialist work in the PRINCE2 project. It will be part of the text in the Project Initiation Document.

Project records
A collection of all approved management, specialist and quality products and other material, which is necessary to provide an auditable record of the project.

NB. This does not include working files.

Project start-up notification

Advice to the host location that the project is about to start and requesting any required Project Support services.

Project Support Office

A group set up to provide certain administrative services to the Project Manager. Often the group provides its services to many projects in parallel.

Quality

The totality of features and characteristics of a product or service that bear on its ability to satisfy stated and implied needs. Also defined as 'fitness for purpose' or 'conforms to requirements'.

Quality management system

The complete set of quality standards, procedures and responsibilities for a site or organisation.

Quality review

A quality review is a quality checking technique with a specific structure, defined roles and procedure designed to ensure a product's completeness and adherence to standards. The participants are drawn from those with an interest in the product and those with the necessary skills to review its correctness. An example of the checks made by a quality review is 'Does the document match the quality criteria in the Product Description?'

Quality system

See Quality Management System.

Request for Change

A means of proposing a modification to the current specification of a product. It is one type of Project Issue.

Reviewer

A person asked to review a product that is the subject of a quality review.

Risk Log

A document that provides identification, estimation, impact evaluation and countermeasures for all risks to the project. It should be created during the start-up of the project and developed during the life of the project. Also known as 'Risk Register'.

Risk profile

A graphical representation of information normally found on the Risk Log.

Risk Register

See Risk Log.

Senior Responsible Owner
This is not a PRINCE2 term, but is used in many organisations. Its equivalent in PRINCE2 terms would be the 'Executive' role.

Senior Supplier
The Project Board role that provides knowledge and experience of the main discipline(s) involved in the production of the project's deliverable(s). Represents the supplier(s) interests within the project and provides supplier resources.

Senior User
A member of the Project Board, accountable for ensuring that user needs are specified correctly and that the solution meets those needs.

Sponsor
Not a specific PRINCE2 role but often used to mean the major driving force of a project. May be the equivalent of 'Executive' or corporate/programme management.

Stakeholders
Parties with an interest in the execution and outcome of a project. They would include business streams affected by or dependent on the outcome of a project.

Supplier
The group or groups responsible for the supply of the project's specialist products.

Team Manager
A role that may be employed by the Project Manager or a specifically appointed alternative person to manage the work of project team members.

Tolerance
The permissible deviation above and below a plan's estimate of time and cost without escalating the deviation to the next level of management. Separate Tolerance figures should be given for time and cost. There may also be Tolerance levels for quality, scope, benefit and risk. Tolerance is applied at project, stage and team levels.

User(s)
The person or group who will use the final deliverable(s) of the project.

Work Package
The set of information relevant to the creation of one or more products. It will contain the Product Description(s), details of any constraints on production such as time and cost, interfaces and confirmation of the agreement between the Project Manager and the person or Team Manager who is to implement the Work Package that the work can be done within the constraints.

INDEX

Note: The index does not contain references to the Glossary.